R Programming for Data Science

Roger D. Peng

R Programming for Data Science

Roger D. Peng

ISBN 978-1-365-05682-6

This is a Leanpub book. Leanpub empowers authors and publishers with the Lean Publishing process. Lean Publishing is the act of publishing an in-progress ebook using lightweight tools and many iterations to get reader feedback, pivot until you have the right book and build traction once you do.

© 2014 - 2016 Roger D. Peng

Also By Roger D. Peng

The Art of Data Science

Exploratory Data Analysis with R

Report Writing for Data Science in R

Contents

1. Stay in Touch! 1
2. Preface 3
3. History and Overview of R 7
   3.1   What is R? 7
   3.2   What is S? 7
   3.3   The S Philosophy 8
   3.4   Back to R 8
   3.5   Basic Features of R 9
   3.6   Free Software 9
   3.7   Design of the R System 10
   3.8   Limitations of R 11
   3.9   R Resources 12
4. Getting Started with R 15
   4.1   Installation 15
   4.2   Getting started with the R interface 15
5. R Nuts and Bolts 17
   5.1   Entering Input 17
   5.2   Evaluation 17
   5.3   R Objects 18
   5.4   Numbers 19
   5.5   Attributes 19
   5.6   Creating Vectors 19
   5.7   Mixing Objects 20
   5.8   Explicit Coercion 20
   5.9   Matrices 21
   5.10 Lists 22
   5.11 Factors 23
   5.12 Missing Values 24
   5.13 Data Frames 25
   5.14 Names 26

| | | 5.15 | Summary . . . . | 27 |

6. **Getting Data In and Out of R** 29
   - 6.1 Reading and Writing Data 29
   - 6.2 Reading Data Files with `read.table()` 29
   - 6.3 Reading in Larger Datasets with read.table 30
   - 6.4 Calculating Memory Requirements for R Objects 31

7. **Using the `readr` Package** 33

8. **Using Textual and Binary Formats for Storing Data** 35
   - 8.1 Using `dput()` and `dump()` 35
   - 8.2 Binary Formats 37

9. **Interfaces to the Outside World** 39
   - 9.1 File Connections 39
   - 9.2 Reading Lines of a Text File 40
   - 9.3 Reading From a URL Connection 41

10. **Subsetting R Objects** 43
    - 10.1 Subsetting a Vector 43
    - 10.2 Subsetting a Matrix 44
    - 10.3 Subsetting Lists 45
    - 10.4 Subsetting Nested Elements of a List 46
    - 10.5 Extracting Multiple Elements of a List 47
    - 10.6 Partial Matching 47
    - 10.7 Removing NA Values 48

11. **Vectorized Operations** 51
    - 11.1 Vectorized Matrix Operations 52

12. **Dates and Times** 53
    - 12.1 Dates in R 53
    - 12.2 Times in R 53
    - 12.3 Operations on Dates and Times 55
    - 12.4 Summary 56

13. **Managing Data Frames with the `dplyr` package** 57
    - 13.1 Data Frames 57
    - 13.2 The `dplyr` Package 57
    - 13.3 `dplyr` Grammar 58
    - 13.4 Installing the `dplyr` package 58
    - 13.5 `select()` 59
    - 13.6 `filter()` 61
    - 13.7 `arrange()` 63

	13.8	`rename()`	64
	13.9	`mutate()`	65
	13.10	`group_by()`	66
	13.11	`%>%`	67
	13.12	Summary	69

14. Control Structures — 71
- 14.1 `if-else` — 71
- 14.2 `for` Loops — 73
- 14.3 Nested `for` loops — 75
- 14.4 `while` Loops — 75
- 14.5 `repeat` Loops — 76
- 14.6 `next`, `break` — 77
- 14.7 Summary — 78

15. Functions — 79
- 15.1 Functions in R — 79
- 15.2 Your First Function — 79
- 15.3 Argument Matching — 82
- 15.4 Lazy Evaluation — 85
- 15.5 The ... Argument — 85
- 15.6 Arguments Coming After the ... Argument — 86
- 15.7 Summary — 87

16. Scoping Rules of R — 89
- 16.1 A Diversion on Binding Values to Symbol — 89
- 16.2 Scoping Rules — 90
- 16.3 Lexical Scoping: Why Does It Matter? — 91
- 16.4 Lexical vs. Dynamic Scoping — 92
- 16.5 Application: Optimization — 94
- 16.6 Plotting the Likelihood — 96
- 16.7 Summary — 99

17. Coding Standards for R — 101

18. Loop Functions — 103
- 18.1 Looping on the Command Line — 103
- 18.2 `lapply()` — 103
- 18.3 `sapply()` — 107
- 18.4 `split()` — 108
- 18.5 Splitting a Data Frame — 109
- 18.6 `tapply` — 113
- 18.7 `apply()` — 114
- 18.8 Col/Row Sums and Means — 115

	18.9	Other Ways to Apply	116
	18.10	`mapply()`	117
	18.11	Vectorizing a Function	119
	18.12	Summary	120
19.	**Regular Expressions**	**121**
	19.1	Before You Begin	121
	19.2	Primary R Functions	121
	19.3	`grep()`	122
	19.4	`grepl()`	125
	19.5	`regexpr()`	125
	19.6	`sub()` and `gsub()`	127
	19.7	`regexec()`	128
	19.8	Summary	131
20.	**Debugging**	**133**
	20.1	Something's Wrong!	133
	20.2	Figuring Out What's Wrong	136
	20.3	Debugging Tools in R	136
	20.4	Using `traceback()`	137
	20.5	Using `debug()`	138
	20.6	Using `recover()`	139
	20.7	Summary	140
21.	**Profiling R Code**	**141**
	21.1	Using `system.time()`	142
	21.2	Timing Longer Expressions	143
	21.3	The R Profiler	143
	21.4	Using `summaryRprof()`	145
	21.5	Summary	146
22.	**Simulation**	**147**
	22.1	Generating Random Numbers	147
	22.2	Setting the random number seed	148
	22.3	Simulating a Linear Model	149
	22.4	Random Sampling	154
	22.5	Summary	156
23.	**Data Analysis Case Study: Changes in Fine Particle Air Pollution in the U.S.**	**157**
	23.1	Synopsis	157
	23.2	Loading and Processing the Raw Data	157
	23.3	Results	159
24.	**Parallel Computation**	**167**

	24.1	Hidden Parallelism	167
	24.2	Embarrassing Parallelism	169
	24.3	The Parallel Package	170
	24.4	Example: Bootstrapping a Statistic	175
	24.5	Building a Socket Cluster	179
	24.6	Summary	181
25.	About the Author		183

1. Stay in Touch!

Thanks for purchasing this book. If you are interested in hearing more from me about things that I'm working on (books, data science courses, podcast, etc.), you can do two things:

- First, I encourage you to join my mailing list of Leanpub Readers[1]. On this list I send out updates of my own activities as well as occasional comments on data science current events. I'll also let you know what my co-conspirators Jeff Leek and Brian Caffo are up to because sometimes they do really cool stuff.
- Second, I have a regular podcast called Not So Standard Deviations[2] that I co-host with Dr. Hilary Parker, a Data Scientist at Stitch Fix. On this podcast, Hilary and I talk about the craft of data science and discuss common issues and problems in analyzing data. We'll also compare how data science is approached in both academia and industry contexts and discuss the latest industry trends. You can listen to recent episodes on our SoundCloud page or you can subscribe to it in iTunes[3] or your favorite podcasting app.

For those of you who purchased a **printed copy** of this book, I encourage you to go to the Leanpub web site and obtain the e-book version[4], which is available for free. The reason is that I will occasionally update the book with new material and readers who purchase the e-book version are entitled to free updates (this is unfortunately not yet possible with printed books).

Thanks again for purchasing this book and please do stay in touch!

---

[1] http://eepurl.com/bAJ3zj
[2] https://soundcloud.com/nssd-podcast
[3] https://itunes.apple.com/us/podcast/not-so-standard-deviations/id1040614570
[4] https://leanpub.com/rprogramming

2. Preface

I started using R in 1998 when I was a college undergraduate working on my senior thesis. The version was 0.63. I was an applied mathematics major with a statistics concentration and I was working with Dr. Nicolas Hengartner on an analysis of word frequencies in classic texts (Shakespeare, Milton, etc.). The idea was to see if we could identify the authorship of each of the texts based on how frequently they used certain words. We downloaded the data from Project Gutenberg and used some basic linear discriminant analysis for the modeling. The work was eventually published[1] and was my first ever peer-reviewed publication. I guess you could argue it was my first real "data science" experience.

Back then, no one was using R. Most of my classes were taught with Minitab, SPSS, Stata, or Microsoft Excel. The cool people on the cutting edge of statistical methodology used S-PLUS. I was working on my thesis late one night and I had a problem. I didn't have a copy of any of those software packages because they were expensive and I was a student. I didn't feel like trekking over to the computer lab to use the software because it was late at night.

But I had the Internet! After a couple of Yahoo! searches I found a web page for something called R, which I figured was just a play on the name of the S-PLUS package. From what I could tell, R was a "clone" of S-PLUS that was free. I had already written some S-PLUS code for my thesis so I figured I would try to download R and see if I could just run the S-PLUS code.

It didn't work. At least not at first. It turns out that R is not exactly a clone of S-PLUS and quite a few modifications needed to be made before the code would run in R. In particular, R was missing a lot of statistical functionality that had existed in S-PLUS for a long time already. Luckily, R's programming language was pretty much there and I was able to more or less re-implement the features that were missing in R.

After college, I enrolled in a PhD program in statistics at the University of California, Los Angeles. At the time the department was brand new and they didn't have a lot of policies or rules (or classes, for that matter!). So you could kind of do what you wanted, which was good for some students and not so good for others. The Chair of the department, Jan de Leeuw, was a big fan of XLisp-Stat and so all of the department's classes were taught using XLisp-Stat. I diligently bought my copy of Luke Tierney's book[2] and learned to really love XLisp-Stat. It had a number of features that R didn't have at all, most notably dynamic graphics.

But ultimately, there were only so many parentheses that I could type, and still all of the research-level statistics was being done in S-PLUS. The department didn't really have a lot of copies of S-PLUS lying around so I turned back to R. When I looked around at my fellow students, I realized that I was basically the only one who had any experience using R. Since there was a budding interest in R

---

[1] http://amstat.tandfonline.com/doi/abs/10.1198/000313002100#.VQGiSELpagE
[2] http://www.amazon.com/LISP-STAT-Object-Oriented-Environment-Statistical-Probability/dp/0471509167/

around the department, I decided to start a "brown bag" series where every week for about an hour I would talk about something you could do in R (which wasn't much, really). People seemed to like it, if only because there wasn't really anyone to turn to if you wanted to learn about R.

By the time I left grad school in 2003, the department had essentially switched over from XLisp-Stat to R for all its work (although there were a few hold outs). Jan discusses the rationale for the transition in a paper[3] in the *Journal of Statistical Software*.

In the next step of my career, I went to the Department of Biostatistics[4] at the Johns Hopkins Bloomberg School of Public Health, where I have been for the past 12 years. When I got to Johns Hopkins people already seemed into R. Most people had abandoned S-PLUS a while ago and were committed to using R for their research. Of all the available statistical packages, R had the most powerful and expressive programming language, which was perfect for someone developing *new* statistical methods.

However, we didn't really have a class that taught students how to use R. This was a problem because most of our grad students were coming into the program having never heard of R. Most likely in their undergradute programs, they used some other software package. So along with Rafael Irizarry, Brian Caffo, Ingo Ruczinski, and Karl Broman, I started a new class to teach our graduate students R and a number of other skills they'd need in grad school.

The class was basically a weekly seminar where one of us talked about a computing topic of interest. I gave some of the R lectures in that class and when I asked people who had heard of R before, almost no one raised their hand. And no one had actually used it before. The main selling point at the time was "It's just like S-PLUS but it's free!" A lot of people had experience with SAS or Stata or SPSS. A number of people had used something like Java or C/C++ before and so I often used that a reference frame. No one had ever used a functional-style of programming language like Scheme or Lisp.

To this day, I still teach the class, known a Biostatistics 140.776 ("Statistical Computing"). However, the nature of the class has changed quite a bit over the past 10 years. The population of students (mostly first-year graduate students) has shifted to the point where many of them have been introduced to R as undergraduates. This trend mirrors the overall trend with statistics where we are seeing more and more students do undergraduate majors in statistics (as opposed to, say, mathematics). Eventually, by 2008–2009, when I'd asked how many people had heard of or used R before, everyone raised their hand. However, even at that late date, I still felt the need to convince people that R was a "real" language that could be used for real tasks.

R has grown a lot in recent years, and is being used in so many places now, that I think it's essentially impossible for a person to keep track of everything that is going on. That's fine, but it makes "introducing" people to R an interesting experience. Nowadays in class, students are often teaching me something new about R that I've never seen or heard of before (they are quite good at Googling around for themselves). I feel no need to "bring people over" to R. In fact it's quite the opposite–people might start asking questions if I *weren't* teaching R.

---

[3] http://www.jstatsoft.org/v13/i07
[4] http://www.biostat.jhsph.edu

This book comes from my experience teaching R in a variety of settings and through different stages of its (and my) development. Much of the material has been taken from by Statistical Computing class as well as the R Programming[5] class I teach through Coursera.

I'm looking forward to teaching R to people as long as people will let me, and I'm interested in seeing how the next generation of students will approach it (and how my approach to them will change). Overall, it's been just an amazing experience to see the widespread adoption of R over the past decade. I'm sure the next decade will be just as amazing.

---

[5]https://www.coursera.org/course/rprog

3. History and Overview of R

There are only two kinds of languages: the ones people complain about and the ones nobody uses —*Bjarne Stroustrup*

Watch a video of this chapter[1]

3.1 What is R?

This is an easy question to answer. R is a dialect of S.

3.2 What is S?

S is a language that was developed by John Chambers and others at the old Bell Telephone Laboratories, originally part of AT&T Corp. S was initiated in 1976[2] as an internal statistical analysis environment—originally implemented as Fortran libraries. Early versions of the language did not even contain functions for statistical modeling.

In 1988 the system was rewritten in C and began to resemble the system that we have today (this was Version 3 of the language). The book *Statistical Models in S* by Chambers and Hastie (the white book) documents the statistical analysis functionality. Version 4 of the S language was released in 1998 and is the version we use today. The book *Programming with Data* by John Chambers (the green book) documents this version of the language.

Since the early 90's the life of the S language has gone down a rather winding path. In 1993 Bell Labs gave StatSci (later Insightful Corp.) an exclusive license to develop and sell the S language. In 2004 Insightful purchased the S language from Lucent for $2 million. In 2006, Alcatel purchased Lucent Technologies and is now called Alcatel-Lucent.

Insightful sold its implementation of the S language under the product name S-PLUS and built a number of fancy features (GUIs, mostly) on top of it—hence the "PLUS". In 2008 Insightful was acquired by TIBCO for $25 million. As of this writing TIBCO is the current owner of the S language and is its exclusive developer.

The fundamentals of the S language itself has not changed dramatically since the publication of the Green Book by John Chambers in 1998. In 1998, S won the Association for Computing Machinery's Software System Award, a highly prestigious award in the computer science field.

---

[1]https://youtu.be/STihTnVSZnI
[2]http://cm.bell-labs.com/stat/doc/94.11.ps

3.3 The S Philosophy

The general S philosophy is important to understand for users of S and R because it sets the stage for the design of the language itself, which many programming veterans find a bit odd and confusing. In particular, it's important to realize that the S language had its roots in data analysis, and did not come from a traditional programming language background. Its inventors were focused on figuring out how to make data analysis easier, first for themselves, and then eventually for others.

In Stages in the Evolution of S[3], John Chambers writes:

> "[W]e wanted users to be able to begin in an interactive environment, where they did not consciously think of themselves as programming. Then as their needs became clearer and their sophistication increased, they should be able to slide gradually into programming, when the language and system aspects would become more important."

The key part here was the transition from *user* to *developer*. They wanted to build a language that could easily service both "people". More technically, they needed to build language that would be suitable for interactive data analysis (more command-line based) as well as for writing longer programs (more traditional programming language-like).

3.4 Back to R

The R language came to use quite a bit after S had been developed. One key limitation of the S language was that it was only available in a commericial package, S-PLUS. In 1991, R was created by Ross Ihaka and Robert Gentleman in the Department of Statistics at the University of Auckland. In 1993 the first announcement of R was made to the public. Ross's and Robert's experience developing R is documented in a 1996 paper in the *Journal of Computational and Graphical Statistics*:

> Ross Ihaka and Robert Gentleman. R: A language for data analysis and graphics. Journal of Computational and Graphical Statistics, 5(3):299–314, 1996

In 1995, Martin Mächler made an important contribution by convincing Ross and Robert to use the GNU General Public License[4] to make R free software. This was critical because it allowed for the source code for the entire R system to be accessible to anyone who wanted to tinker with it (more on free software later).

In 1996, a public mailing list was created (the R-help and R-devel lists) and in 1997 the R Core Group was formed, containing some people associated with S and S-PLUS. Currently, the core group controls the source code for R and is solely able to check in changes to the main R source tree. Finally, in 2000 R version 1.0.0 was released to the public.

---

[3] http://www.stat.bell-labs.com/S/history.html
[4] http://www.gnu.org/licenses/gpl-2.0.html

3.5 Basic Features of R

In the early days, a key feature of R was that its syntax is very similar to S, making it easy for S-PLUS users to switch over. While the R's syntax is nearly identical to that of S's, R's semantics, while superficially similar to S, are quite different. In fact, R is technically much closer to the Scheme language than it is to the original S language when it comes to how R works under the hood.

Today R runs on almost any standard computing platform and operating system. Its open source nature means that anyone is free to adapt the software to whatever platform they choose. Indeed, R has been reported to be running on modern tablets, phones, PDAs, and game consoles.

One nice feature that R shares with many popular open source projects is frequent releases. These days there is a major annual release, typically in October, where major new features are incorporated and released to the public. Throughout the year, smaller-scale bugfix releases will be made as needed. The frequent releases and regular release cycle indicates active development of the software and ensures that bugs will be addressed in a timely manner. Of course, while the core developers control the primary source tree for R, many people around the world make contributions in the form of new feature, bug fixes, or both.

Another key advantage that R has over many other statistical packages (even today) is its sophisticated graphics capabilities. R's ability to create "publication quality" graphics has existed since the very beginning and has generally been better than competing packages. Today, with many more visualization packages available than before, that trend continues. R's base graphics system allows for very fine control over essentially every aspect of a plot or graph. Other newer graphics systems, like lattice and ggplot2 allow for complex and sophisticated visualizations of high-dimensional data.

R has maintained the original S philosophy, which is that it provides a language that is both useful for interactive work, but contains a powerful programming language for developing new tools. This allows the user, who takes existing tools and applies them to data, to slowly but surely become a developer who is creating new tools.

Finally, one of the joys of using R has nothing to do with the language itself, but rather with the active and vibrant user community. In many ways, a language is successful inasmuch as it creates a platform with which many people can create new things. R is that platform and thousands of people around the world have come together to make contributions to R, to develop packages, and help each other use R for all kinds of applications. The R-help and R-devel mailing lists have been highly active for over a decade now and there is considerable activity on web sites like Stack Overflow.

3.6 Free Software

A major advantage that R has over many other statistical packages and is that it's free in the sense of free software (it's also free in the sense of free beer). The copyright for the primary source code for R is held by the R Foundation[5] and is published under the GNU General Public License version

---
[5]http://www.r-project.org/foundation/

2.0[6].

According to the Free Software Foundation, with *free software*, you are granted the following four freedoms[7]

- The freedom to run the program, for any purpose (freedom 0).
- The freedom to study how the program works, and adapt it to your needs (freedom 1). Access to the source code is a precondition for this.
- The freedom to redistribute copies so you can help your neighbor (freedom 2).
- The freedom to improve the program, and release your improvements to the public, so that the whole community benefits (freedom 3). Access to the source code is a precondition for this.

You can visit the Free Software Foundation's web site[8] to learn a lot more about free software. The Free Software Foundation was founded by Richard Stallman in 1985 and Stallman's personal web site[9] is an interesting read if you happen to have some spare time.

3.7 Design of the R System

The primary R system is available from the Comprehensive R Archive Network[10], also known as CRAN. CRAN also hosts many add-on packages that can be used to extend the functionality of R.

The R system is divided into 2 conceptual parts:

1. The "base" R system that you download from CRAN: Linux[11] Windows[12] Mac[13] Source Code[14]
2. Everything else.

R functionality is divided into a number of *packages*.

- The "base" R system contains, among other things, the base package which is required to run R and contains the most fundamental functions.
- The other packages contained in the "base" system include utils, stats, datasets, graphics, grDevices, grid, methods, tools, parallel, compiler, splines, tcltk, stats4.

---

[6] http://www.gnu.org/licenses/gpl-2.0.html
[7] http://www.gnu.org/philosophy/free-sw.html
[8] http://www.fsf.org
[9] https://stallman.org
[10] http://cran.r-project.org
[11] http://cran.r-project.org/bin/linux/
[12] http://cran.r-project.org/bin/windows/
[13] http://cran.r-project.org/bin/macosx/
[14] http://cran.r-project.org/src/base/R-3/R-3.1.3.tar.gz

- There are also "Recommended" packages: `boot`, `class`, `cluster`, `codetools`, `foreign`, `KernSmooth`, `lattice`, `mgcv`, `nlme`, `rpart`, `survival`, `MASS`, `spatial`, `nnet`, `Matrix`.

When you download a fresh installation of R from CRAN, you get all of the above, which represents a substantial amount of functionality. However, there are many other packages available:

- There are over 4000 packages on CRAN that have been developed by users and programmers around the world.
- There are also many packages associated with the Bioconductor project[15].
- People often make packages available on their personal websites; there is no reliable way to keep track of how many packages are available in this fashion.
- There are a number of packages being developed on repositories like GitHub and BitBucket but there is no reliable listing of all these packages.

3.8 Limitations of R

No programming language or statistical analysis system is perfect. R certainly has a number of drawbacks. For starters, R is essentially based on almost 50 year old technology, going back to the original S system developed at Bell Labs. There was originally little built in support for dynamic or 3-D graphics (but things have improved greatly since the "old days").

Another commonly cited limitation of R is that objects must generally be stored in physical memory. This is in part due to the scoping rules of the language, but R generally is more of a memory hog than other statistical packages. However, there have been a number of advancements to deal with this, both in the R core and also in a number of packages developed by contributors. Also, computing power and capacity has continued to grow over time and amount of physical memory that can be installed on even a consumer-level laptop is substantial. While we will likely never have enough physical memory on a computer to handle the increasingly large datasets that are being generated, the situation has gotten quite a bit easier over time.

At a higher level one "limitation" of R is that its functionality is based on consumer demand and (voluntary) user contributions. If no one feels like implementing your favorite method, then it's *your* job to implement it (or you need to pay someone to do it). The capabilities of the R system generally reflect the interests of the R user community. As the community has ballooned in size over the past 10 years, the capabilities have similarly increased. When I first started using R, there was very little in the way of functionality for the physical sciences (physics, astronomy, etc.). However, now some of those communities have adopted R and we are seeing more code being written for those kinds of applications.

If you want to know my general views on the usefulness of R, you can see them here in the following exchange on the R-help mailing list with Douglas Bates and Brian Ripley in June 2004:

---

[15] http://bioconductor.org

Roger D. Peng: I don't think anyone actually believes that R is designed to make *everyone* happy. For me, R does about 99% of the things I need to do, but sadly, when I need to order a pizza, I still have to pick up the telephone.

Douglas Bates: There are several chains of pizzerias in the U.S. that provide for Internet-based ordering (e.g. www.papajohnsonline.com) so, with the Internet modules in R, it's only a matter of time before you will have a pizza-ordering function available.

Brian D. Ripley: Indeed, the GraphApp toolkit (used for the RGui interface under R for Windows, but Guido forgot to include it) provides one (for use in Sydney, Australia, we presume as that is where the GraphApp author hails from). Alternatively, a Padovian has no need of ordering pizzas with both home and neighbourhood restaurants ....

At this point in time, I think it would be fairly straightforward to build a pizza ordering R package using something like the `RCurl` or `httr` packages. Any takers?

3.9 R Resources

Official Manuals

As far as getting started with R by reading stuff, there is of course this book. Also, available from CRAN[16] are

- An Introduction to R[17]
- R Data Import/Export[18]
- Writing R Extensions[19]: Discusses how to write and organize R packages
- R Installation and Administration[20]: This is mostly for building R from the source code)
- R Internals[21]: This manual describes the low level structure of R and is primarily for developers and R core members
- R Language Definition[22]: This documents the R language and, again, is primarily for developers

---

[16] http://cran.r-project.org
[17] http://cran.r-project.org/doc/manuals/r-release/R-intro.html
[18] http://cran.r-project.org/doc/manuals/r-release/R-data.html
[19] http://cran.r-project.org/doc/manuals/r-release/R-exts.html
[20] http://cran.r-project.org/doc/manuals/r-release/R-admin.html
[21] http://cran.r-project.org/doc/manuals/r-release/R-ints.html
[22] http://cran.r-project.org/doc/manuals/r-release/R-lang.html

Useful Standard Texts on S and R

- Chambers (2008). *Software for Data Analysis*, Springer
- Chambers (1998). *Programming with Data*, Springer: This book is *not* about R, but it describes the organization and philosophy of the current version of the S language, and is a useful reference.
- Venables & Ripley (2002). *Modern Applied Statistics with S*, Springer: This is a standard textbook in statistics and describes how to use many statistical methods in R. This book has an associated R package (the MASS package) that comes with every installation of R.
- Venables & Ripley (2000). *S Programming*, Springer: This book is a little old but is still relevant and accurate. Despite its title, this book is useful for R also.
- Murrell (2005). *R Graphics*, Chapman & Hall/CRC Press: Paul Murrell wrote and designed much of the graphics system in R and this book essentially documents the underlying details. This is not so much a "user-level" book as a developer-level book. But it is an important book for anyone interested in designing new types of graphics or visualizations.
- Wickham (2014). *Advanced R*, Chapman & Hall/CRC Press: This book by Hadley Wickham covers a number of areas including object-oriented programming, functional programming, profiling and other advanced topics.

Other Resources

- Major technical publishers like Springer, Chapman & Hall/CRC have entire series of books dedicated to using R in various applications. For example, Springer has a series of books called *Use R!*.
- A longer list of books can be found on the CRAN web site[23].

---

[23] http://www.r-project.org/doc/bib/R-books.html

4. Getting Started with R

4.1 Installation

The first thing you need to do to get started with R is to install it on your computer. R works on pretty much every platform available, including the widely available Windows, Mac OS X, and Linux systems. If you want to watch a step-by-step tutorial on how to install R for Mac or Windows, you can watch these videos:

- Installing R on Windows[1]
- Installing R on the Mac[2]

There is also an integrated development environment available for R that is built by RStudio. I really like this IDE—it has a nice editor with syntax highlighting, there is an R object viewer, and there are a number of other nice features that are integrated. You can see how to install RStudio here

- Installing RStudio[3]

The RStudio IDE is available from RStudio's web site[4].

4.2 Getting started with the R interface

After you install R you will need to launch it and start writing R code. Before we get to exactly how to write R code, it's useful to get a sense of how the system is organized. In these two videos I talk about where to write code and how set your working directory, which let's R know where to find all of your files.

- Writing code and setting your working directory on the Mac[5]
- Writing code and setting your working directory on Windows[6]

---

[1] http://youtu.be/Ohnk9hcxf9M
[2] https://youtu.be/uxuuWXU-7UQ
[3] https://youtu.be/bM7Sfz-LADM
[4] http://rstudio.com
[5] https://youtu.be/8xT3hmJQskU
[6] https://youtu.be/XBcvH1BpIBo

5. R Nuts and Bolts

5.1 Entering Input

Watch a video of this section[1]

At the R prompt we type expressions. The <- symbol is the assignment operator.

```
> x <- 1
> print(x)
[1] 1
> x
[1] 1
> msg <- "hello"
```

The grammar of the language determines whether an expression is complete or not.

```
x <-    ## Incomplete expression
```

The # character indicates a comment. Anything to the right of the # (including the # itself) is ignored. This is the only comment character in R. Unlike some other languages, R does not support multi-line comments or comment blocks.

5.2 Evaluation

When a complete expression is entered at the prompt, it is evaluated and the result of the evaluated expression is returned. The result may be *auto-printed*.

```
> x <- 5   ## nothing printed
> x        ## auto-printing occurs
[1] 5
> print(x) ## explicit printing
[1] 5
```

---
[1]https://youtu.be/vGY5i_J2c-c?t=4m43s

The [1] shown in the output indicates that x is a vector and 5 is its first element.

Typically with interactive work, we do not explicitly print objects with the print function; it is much easier to just auto-print them by typing the name of the object and hitting return/enter. However, when writing scripts, functions, or longer programs, there is sometimes a need to explicitly print objects because auto-printing does not work in those settings.

When an R vector is printed you will notice that an index for the vector is printed in square brackets [] on the side. For example, see this integer sequence of length 20.

```
> x <- 11:30
> x
 [1] 11 12 13 14 15 16 17 18 19 20 21 22
[13] 23 24 25 26 27 28 29 30
```

The numbers in the square brackets are not part of the vector itself, they are merely part of the *printed output*.

With R, it's important that one understand that there is a difference between the actual R object and the manner in which that R object is printed to the console. Often, the printed output may have additional bells and whistles to make the output more friendly to the users. However, these bells and whistles are not inherently part of the object.

Note that the : operator is used to create integer sequences.

5.3 R Objects

Watch a video of this section[2]

R has five basic or "atomic" classes of objects:

- character
- numeric (real numbers)
- integer
- complex
- logical (True/False)

The most basic type of R object is a vector. Empty vectors can be created with the vector() function. There is really only one rule about vectors in R, which is that **A vector can only contain objects of the same class**.

But of course, like any good rule, there is an exception, which is a *list*, which we will get to a bit later. A list is represented as a vector but can contain objects of different classes. Indeed, that's usually why we use them.

There is also a class for "raw" objects, but they are not commonly used directly in data analysis and I won't cover them here.

---
[2]https://youtu.be/vGY5i_J2c-c

5.4 Numbers

Numbers in R are generally treated as numeric objects (i.e. double precision real numbers). This means that even if you see a number like "1" or "2" in R, which you might think of as integers, they are likely represented behind the scenes as numeric objects (so something like "1.00" or "2.00"). This isn't important most of the time…except when it is.

If you explicitly want an integer, you need to specify the L suffix. So entering 1 in R gives you a numeric object; entering 1L explicitly gives you an integer object.

There is also a special number Inf which represents infinity. This allows us to represent entities like 1 / 0. This way, Inf can be used in ordinary calculations; e.g. 1 / Inf is 0.

The value NaN represents an undefined value ("not a number"); e.g. 0 / 0; NaN can also be thought of as a missing value (more on that later)

5.5 Attributes

R objects can have attributes, which are like metadata for the object. These metadata can be very useful in that they help to describe the object. For example, column names on a data frame help to tell us what data are contained in each of the columns. Some examples of R object attributes are

- names, dimnames
- dimensions (e.g. matrices, arrays)
- class (e.g. integer, numeric)
- length
- other user-defined attributes/metadata

Attributes of an object (if any) can be accessed using the attributes() function. Not all R objects contain attributes, in which case the attributes() function returns NULL.

5.6 Creating Vectors

Watch a video of this section[3]

The c() function can be used to create vectors of objects by concatenating things together.

---

[3]https://youtu.be/w8_XdYI3reU

```
> x <- c(0.5, 0.6)       ## numeric
> x <- c(TRUE, FALSE)    ## logical
> x <- c(T, F)           ## logical
> x <- c("a", "b", "c")  ## character
> x <- 9:29              ## integer
> x <- c(1+0i, 2+4i)     ## complex
```

Note that in the above example, T and F are short-hand ways to specify TRUE and FALSE. However, in general one should try to use the explicit TRUE and FALSE values when indicating logical values. The T and F values are primarily there for when you're feeling lazy.

You can also use the vector() function to initialize vectors.

```
> x <- vector("numeric", length = 10)
> x
 [1] 0 0 0 0 0 0 0 0 0 0
```

5.7 Mixing Objects

There are occasions when different classes of R objects get mixed together. Sometimes this happens by accident but it can also happen on purpose. So what happens with the following code?

```
> y <- c(1.7, "a")   ## character
> y <- c(TRUE, 2)    ## numeric
> y <- c("a", TRUE)  ## character
```

In each case above, we are mixing objects of two different classes in a vector. But remember that the only rule about vectors says this is not allowed. When different objects are mixed in a vector, *coercion* occurs so that every element in the vector is of the same class.

In the example above, we see the effect of *implicit coercion*. What R tries to do is find a way to represent all of the objects in the vector in a reasonable fashion. Sometimes this does exactly what you want and...sometimes not. For example, combining a numeric object with a character object will create a character vector, because numbers can usually be easily represented as strings.

5.8 Explicit Coercion

Objects can be explicitly coerced from one class to another using the as.* functions, if available.

```
> x <- 0:6
> class(x)
[1] "integer"
> as.numeric(x)
[1] 0 1 2 3 4 5 6
> as.logical(x)
[1] FALSE  TRUE  TRUE  TRUE  TRUE  TRUE  TRUE
> as.character(x)
[1] "0" "1" "2" "3" "4" "5" "6"
```

Sometimes, R can't figure out how to coerce an object and this can result in NAs being produced.

```
> x <- c("a", "b", "c")
> as.numeric(x)
Warning: NAs introduced by coercion
[1] NA NA NA
> as.logical(x)
[1] NA NA NA
> as.complex(x)
Warning: NAs introduced by coercion
[1] NA NA NA
```

When nonsensical coercion takes place, you will usually get a warning from R.

5.9 Matrices

Matrices are vectors with a *dimension* attribute. The dimension attribute is itself an integer vector of length 2 (number of rows, number of columns)

```
> m <- matrix(nrow = 2, ncol = 3)
> m
     [,1] [,2] [,3]
[1,]   NA   NA   NA
[2,]   NA   NA   NA
> dim(m)
[1] 2 3
> attributes(m)
$dim
[1] 2 3
```

Matrices are constructed *column-wise*, so entries can be thought of starting in the "upper left" corner and running down the columns.

```
> m <- matrix(1:6, nrow = 2, ncol = 3)
> m
     [,1] [,2] [,3]
[1,]    1    3    5
[2,]    2    4    6
```

Matrices can also be created directly from vectors by adding a dimension attribute.

```
> m <- 1:10
> m
 [1]  1  2  3  4  5  6  7  8  9 10
> dim(m) <- c(2, 5)
> m
     [,1] [,2] [,3] [,4] [,5]
[1,]    1    3    5    7    9
[2,]    2    4    6    8   10
```

Matrices can be created by *column-binding* or *row-binding* with the `cbind()` and `rbind()` functions.

```
> x <- 1:3
> y <- 10:12
> cbind(x, y)
     x  y
[1,] 1 10
[2,] 2 11
[3,] 3 12
> rbind(x, y)
  [,1] [,2] [,3]
x    1    2    3
y   10   11   12
```

5.10 Lists

Lists are a special type of vector that can contain elements of different classes. Lists are a very important data type in R and you should get to know them well. Lists, in combination with the various "apply" functions discussed later, make for a powerful combination.

Lists can be explicitly created using the `list()` function, which takes an arbitrary number of arguments.

```
> x <- list(1, "a", TRUE, 1 + 4i)
> x
[[1]]
[1] 1

[[2]]
[1] "a"

[[3]]
[1] TRUE

[[4]]
[1] 1+4i
```

We can also create an empty list of a prespecified length with the vector() function

```
> x <- vector("list", length = 5)
> x
[[1]]
NULL

[[2]]
NULL

[[3]]
NULL

[[4]]
NULL

[[5]]
NULL
```

5.11 Factors

Watch a video of this section[4]

Factors are used to represent categorical data and can be unordered or ordered. One can think of a factor as an integer vector where each integer has a *label*. Factors are important in statistical modeling and are treated specially by modelling functions like lm() and glm().

Using factors with labels is *better* than using integers because factors are self-describing. Having a variable that has values "Male" and "Female" is better than a variable that has values 1 and 2.

Factor objects can be created with the factor() function.

---
[4]https://youtu.be/NuY6jY4qE7I

```
> x <- factor(c("yes", "yes", "no", "yes", "no"))
> x
[1] yes yes no  yes no
Levels: no yes
> table(x)
x
 no yes
  2   3
> ## See the underlying representation of factor
> unclass(x)
[1] 2 2 1 2 1
attr(,"levels")
[1] "no"  "yes"
```

Often factors will be automatically created for you when you read a dataset in using a function like read.table(). Those functions often default to creating factors when they encounter data that look like characters or strings.

The order of the levels of a factor can be set using the levels argument to factor(). This can be important in linear modelling because the first level is used as the baseline level.

```
> x <- factor(c("yes", "yes", "no", "yes", "no"))
> x  ## Levels are put in alphabetical order
[1] yes yes no  yes no
Levels: no yes
> x <- factor(c("yes", "yes", "no", "yes", "no"),
+             levels = c("yes", "no"))
> x
[1] yes yes no  yes no
Levels: yes no
```

5.12 Missing Values

Missing values are denoted by NA or NaN for q undefined mathematical operations.

- is.na() is used to test objects if they are NA
- is.nan() is used to test for NaN
- NA values have a class also, so there are integer NA, character NA, etc.
- A NaN value is also NA but the converse is not true

```
> ## Create a vector with NAs in it
> x <- c(1, 2, NA, 10, 3)
> ## Return a logical vector indicating which elements are NA
> is.na(x)
[1] FALSE FALSE  TRUE FALSE FALSE
> ## Return a logical vector indicating which elements are NaN
> is.nan(x)
[1] FALSE FALSE FALSE FALSE FALSE


> ## Now create a vector with both NA and NaN values
> x <- c(1, 2, NaN, NA, 4)
> is.na(x)
[1] FALSE FALSE  TRUE  TRUE FALSE
> is.nan(x)
[1] FALSE FALSE  TRUE FALSE FALSE
```

5.13 Data Frames

Data frames are used to store tabular data in R. They are an important type of object in R and are used in a variety of statistical modeling applications. Hadley Wickham's package dplyr[5] has an optimized set of functions designed to work efficiently with data frames.

Data frames are represented as a special type of list where every element of the list has to have the same length. Each element of the list can be thought of as a column and the length of each element of the list is the number of rows.

Unlike matrices, data frames can store different classes of objects in each column. Matrices must have every element be the same class (e.g. all integers or all numeric).

In addition to column names, indicating the names of the variables or predictors, data frames have a special attribute called row.names which indicate information about each row of the data frame.

Data frames are usually created by reading in a dataset using the read.table() or read.csv(). However, data frames can also be created explicitly with the data.frame() function or they can be coerced from other types of objects like lists.

Data frames can be converted to a matrix by calling data.matrix(). While it might seem that the as.matrix() function should be used to coerce a data frame to a matrix, almost always, what you want is the result of data.matrix().

---

[5]https://github.com/hadley/dplyr

```
> x <- data.frame(foo = 1:4, bar = c(T, T, F, F))
> x
  foo   bar
1   1  TRUE
2   2  TRUE
3   3 FALSE
4   4 FALSE
> nrow(x)
[1] 4
> ncol(x)
[1] 2
```

5.14 Names

R objects can have names, which is very useful for writing readable code and self-describing objects. Here is an example of assigning names to an integer vector.

```
> x <- 1:3
> names(x)
NULL
> names(x) <- c("New York", "Seattle", "Los Angeles")
> x
   New York     Seattle Los Angeles
          1           2           3
> names(x)
[1] "New York"    "Seattle"     "Los Angeles"
```

Lists can also have names, which is often very useful.

```
> x <- list("Los Angeles" = 1, Boston = 2, London = 3)
> x
$`Los Angeles`
[1] 1

$Boston
[1] 2

$London
[1] 3
> names(x)
[1] "Los Angeles" "Boston"      "London"
```

Matrices can have both column and row names.

```
> m <- matrix(1:4, nrow = 2, ncol = 2)
> dimnames(m) <- list(c("a", "b"), c("c", "d"))
> m
  c d
a 1 3
b 2 4
```

Column names and row names can be set separately using the `colnames()` and `rownames()` functions.

```
> colnames(m) <- c("h", "f")
> rownames(m) <- c("x", "z")
> m
  h f
x 1 3
z 2 4
```

Note that for data frames, there is a separate function for setting the row names, the `row.names()` function. Also, data frames do not have column names, they just have names (like lists). So to set the column names of a data frame just use the `names()` function. Yes, I know its confusing. Here's a quick summary:

Object	Set column names	Set row names
data frame	names()	row.names()
matrix	colnames()	rownames()

5.15 Summary

There are a variety of different builtin-data types in R. In this chapter we have reviewed the following

- atomic classes: numeric, logical, character, integer, complex
- vectors, lists
- factors
- missing values
- data frames and matrices

All R objects can have attributes that help to describe what is in the object. Perhaps the most useful attribute is names, such as column and row names in a data frame, or simply names in a vector or list. Attributes like dimensions are also important as they can modify the behavior of objects, like turning a vector into a matrix.

6. Getting Data In and Out of R

6.1 Reading and Writing Data

Watch a video of this section[1]

There are a few principal functions reading data into R.

- `read.table`, `read.csv`, for reading tabular data
- `readLines`, for reading lines of a text file
- `source`, for reading in R code files (*inverse of* `dump`)
- `dget`, for reading in R code files (*inverse of* `dput`)
- `load`, for reading in saved workspaces
- `unserialize`, for reading single R objects in binary form

There are of course, many R packages that have been developed to read in all kinds of other datasets, and you may need to resort to one of these packages if you are working in a specific area.

There are analogous functions for writing data to files

- `write.table`, for writing tabular data to text files (i.e. CSV) or connections
- `writeLines`, for writing character data line-by-line to a file or connection
- `dump`, for dumping a textual representation of multiple R objects
- `dput`, for outputting a textual representation of an R object
- `save`, for saving an arbitrary number of R objects in binary format (possibly compressed) to a file.
- `serialize`, for converting an R object into a binary format for outputting to a connection (or file).

6.2 Reading Data Files with `read.table()`

The `read.table()` function is one of the most commonly used functions for reading data. The help file for `read.table()` is worth reading in its entirety if only because the function gets used a lot (run `?read.table` in R). I know, I know, everyone always says to read the help file, but this one is actually worth reading.

The `read.table()` function has a few important arguments:

---

[1]https://youtu.be/Z_dc_FADyi4

- `file`, the name of a file, or a connection
- `header`, logical indicating if the file has a header line
- `sep`, a string indicating how the columns are separated
- `colClasses`, a character vector indicating the class of each column in the dataset
- `nrows`, the number of rows in the dataset. By default `read.table()` reads an entire file.
- `comment.char`, a character string indicating the comment character. This defalts to `"#"`. If there are no commented lines in your file, it's worth setting this to be the empty string `""`.
- `skip`, the number of lines to skip from the beginning
- `stringsAsFactors`, should character variables be coded as factors? This defaults to `TRUE` because back in the old days, if you had data that were stored as strings, it was because those strings represented levels of a categorical variable. Now we have lots of data that is text data and they don't always represent categorical variables. So you may want to set this to be `FALSE` in those cases. If you *always* want this to be `FALSE`, you can set a global option via `options(stringsAsFactors = FALSE)`. I've never seen so much heat generated on discussion forums about an R function argument than the `stringsAsFactors` argument. Seriously.

For small to moderately sized datasets, you can usually call read.table without specifying any other arguments

```
> data <- read.table("foo.txt")
```

In this case, R will automatically

- skip lines that begin with a #
- figure out how many rows there are (and how much memory needs to be allocated)
- figure what type of variable is in each column of the table.

Telling R all these things directly makes R run faster and more efficiently. The `read.csv()` function is identical to read.table except that some of the defaults are set differently (like the `sep` argument).

6.3 Reading in Larger Datasets with read.table

Watch a video of this section[2]

With much larger datasets, there are a few things that you can do that will make your life easier and will prevent R from choking.

- Read the help page for read.table, which contains many hints

---
[2] https://youtu.be/BJYYIJO3UFI

- Make a rough calculation of the memory required to store your dataset (see the next section for an example of how to do this). If the dataset is larger than the amount of RAM on your computer, you can probably stop right here.
- Set comment.char = "" if there are no commented lines in your file.
- Use the colClasses argument. Specifying this option instead of using the default can make 'read.table' run MUCH faster, often twice as fast. In order to use this option, you have to know the class of each column in your data frame. If all of the columns are "numeric", for example, then you can just set colClasses = "numeric". A quick an dirty way to figure out the classes of each column is the following:

```
> initial <- read.table("datatable.txt", nrows = 100)
> classes <- sapply(initial, class)
> tabAll <- read.table("datatable.txt", colClasses = classes)
```

- Set nrows. This doesn't make R run faster but it helps with memory usage. A mild overestimate is okay. You can use the Unix tool wc to calculate the number of lines in a file.

In general, when using R with larger datasets, it's also useful to know a few things about your system.

- How much memory is available on your system?
- What other applications are in use? Can you close any of them?
- Are there other users logged into the same system?
- What operating system ar you using? Some operating systems can limit the amount of memory a single process can access

6.4 Calculating Memory Requirements for R Objects

Because R stores all of its objects physical memory, it is important to be cognizant of how much memory is being used up by all of the data objects residing in your workspace. One situation where it's particularly important to understand memory requirements is when you are reading in a new dataset into R. Fortunately, it's easy to make a back of the envelope calculation of how much memory will be required by a new dataset.

For example, suppose I have a data frame with 1,500,000 rows and 120 columns, all of which are numeric data. Roughly, how much memory is required to store this data frame? Well, on most modern computers double precision floating point numbers[3] are stored using 64 bits of memory, or 8 bytes. Given that information, you can do the following calculation

---
[3]http://en.wikipedia.org/wiki/Double-precision_floating-point_format

$$1{,}500{,}000 \times 120 \times 8 \text{ bytes/numeric} = 1{,}440{,}000{,}000 \text{ bytes}$$
$$= 1{,}440{,}000{,}000 \,/\, 2^{20} \text{ bytes/MB}$$
$$= 1{,}373.29 \text{ MB}$$
$$= 1.34 \text{ GB}$$

So the dataset would require about 1.34 GB of RAM. Most computers these days have at least that much RAM. However, you need to be aware of

- what other programs might be running on your computer, using up RAM
- what other R objects might already be taking up RAM in your workspace

Reading in a large dataset for which you do not have enough RAM is one easy way to freeze up your computer (or at least your R session). This is usually an unpleasant experience that usually requires you to kill the R process, in the best case scenario, or reboot your computer, in the worst case. So make sure to do a rough calculation of memeory requirements before reading in a large dataset. You'll thank me later.

7. Using the `readr` Package

The `readr` package is recently developed by Hadley Wickham to deal with reading in large flat files quickly. The package provides replacements for functions like `read.table()` and `read.csv()`. The analogous functions in `readr` are `read_table()` and `read_csv()`. These functions are often *much* faster than their base R analogues and provide a few other nice features such as progress meters.

For the most part, you can read use `read_table()` and `read_csv()` pretty much anywhere you might use `read.table()` and `read.csv()`. In addition, if there are non-fatal problems that occur while reading in the data, you will get a warning and the returned data frame will have some information about which rows/observations triggered the warning. This can be very helpful for "debugging" problems with your data before you get neck deep in data analysis.

8. Using Textual and Binary Formats for Storing Data

Watch a video of this chapter[1]

There are a variety of ways that data can be stored, including structured text files like CSV or tab-delimited, or more complex binary formats. However, there is an intermediate format that is textual, but not as simple as something like CSV. The format is native to R and is somewhat readable because of its textual nature.

One can create a more descriptive representation of an R object by using the dput() or dump() functions. The dump() and dput() functions are useful because the resulting textual format is editable, and in the case of corruption, potentially recoverable. Unlike writing out a table or CSV file, dump() and dput() preserve the *metadata* (sacrificing some readability), so that another user doesn't have to specify it all over again. For example, we can preserve the class of each column of a table or the levels of a factor variable.

Textual formats can work much better with version control programs like subversion or git which can only track changes meaningfully in text files. In addition, textual formats can be longer-lived; if there is corruption somewhere in the file, it can be easier to fix the problem because one can just open the file in an editor and look at it (although this would probably only be done in a worst case scenario!). Finally, textual formats adhere to the Unix philosophy[2], if that means anything to you.

There are a few downsides to using these intermediate textual formats. The format is not very space-efficient, because all of the metadata is specified. Also, it is really only partially readable. In some instances it might be preferable to have data stored in a CSV file and then have a separate code file that specifies the metadata.

8.1 Using dput() and dump()

One way to pass data around is by deparsing the R object with dput() and reading it back in (parsing it) using dget().

---

[1]https://youtu.be/5mIPigbNDfk
[2]http://www.catb.org/esr/writings/taoup/

```
> ## Create a data frame
> y <- data.frame(a = 1, b = "a")
> ## Print 'dput' output to console
> dput(y)
structure(list(a = 1, b = structure(1L, .Label = "a", class = "factor")), .Names = c("a",
"b"), row.names = c(NA, -1L), class = "data.frame")
```

Notice that the dput() output is in the form of R code and that it preserves metadata like the class of the object, the row names, and the column names.

The output of dput() can also be saved directly to a file.

```
> ## Send 'dput' output to a file
> dput(y, file = "y.R")
> ## Read in 'dput' output from a file
> new.y <- dget("y.R")
> new.y
  a b
1 1 a
```

Multiple objects can be deparsed at once using the dump function and read back in using source.

```
> x <- "foo"
> y <- data.frame(a = 1L, b = "a")
```

We can dump() R objects to a file by passing a character vector of their names.

```
> dump(c("x", "y"), file = "data.R")
> rm(x, y)
```

The inverse of dump() is source().

```
> source("data.R")
> str(y)
'data.frame':    1 obs. of  2 variables:
 $ a: int 1
 $ b: Factor w/ 1 level "a": 1
> x
[1] "foo"
```

8.2 Binary Formats

The complement to the textual format is the binary format, which is sometimes necessary to use for efficiency purposes, or because there's just no useful way to represent data in a textual manner. Also, with numeric data, one can often lose precision when converting to and from a textual format, so it's better to stick with a binary format.

The key functions for converting R objects into a binary format are save(), save.image(), and serialize(). Individual R objects can be saved to a file using the save() function.

```
> a <- data.frame(x = rnorm(100), y = runif(100))
> b <- c(3, 4.4, 1 / 3)
>
> ## Save 'a' and 'b' to a file
> save(a, b, file = "mydata.rda")
>
> ## Load 'a' and 'b' into your workspace
> load("mydata.rda")
```

If you have a lot of objects that you want to save to a file, you can save all objects in your workspace using the save.image() function.

```
> ## Save everything to a file
> save.image(file = "mydata.RData")
>
> ## load all objects in this file
> load("mydata.RData")
```

Notice that I've used the .rda extension when using save() and the .RData extension when using save.image(). This is just my personal preference; you can use whatever file extension you want. The save() and save.image() functions do not care. However, .rda and .RData are fairly common extensions and you may want to use them because they are recognized by other software.

The serialize() function is used to convert individual R objects into a binary format that can be communicated across an arbitrary connection. This may get sent to a file, but it could get sent over a network or other connection.

When you call serialize() on an R object, the output will be a raw vector coded in hexadecimal format.

```
> x <- list(1, 2, 3)
> serialize(x, NULL)
 [1] 58 0a 00 00 00 02 00 03 02 04 00 02 03 00 00 00 00 13 00 00 00 03 00
[24] 00 00 0e 00 00 00 01 3f f0 00 00 00 00 00 00 00 00 00 0e 00 00 00 01
[47] 40 00 00 00 00 00 00 00 00 00 00 0e 00 00 00 01 40 08 00 00 00 00 00
[70] 00
```

If you want, this can be sent to a file, but in that case you are better off using something like save().

The benefit of the serialize() function is that it is the only way to perfectly represent an R object in an exportable format, without losing precision or any metadata. If that is what you need, then serialize() is the function for you.

9. Interfaces to the Outside World

Watch a video of this chapter[1]

Data are read in using *connection* interfaces. Connections can be made to files (most common) or to other more exotic things.

- file, opens a connection to a file
- gzfile, opens a connection to a file compressed with gzip
- bzfile, opens a connection to a file compressed with bzip2
- url, opens a connection to a webpage

In general, connections are powerful tools that let you navigate files or other external objects. Connections can be thought of as a translator that lets you talk to objects that are outside of R. Those outside objects could be anything from a data base, a simple text file, or a a web service API. Connections allow R functions to talk to all these different external objects without you having to write custom code for each object.

9.1 File Connections

Connections to text files can be created with the file() function.

```
> str(file)
function (description = "", open = "", blocking = TRUE, encoding = getOption("encoding"),
    raw = FALSE)
```

The file() function has a number of arguments that are common to many other connection functions so it's worth going into a little detail here.

- description is the name of the file
- open is a code indicating what mode the file should be opened in

The open argument allows for the following options:

- "r" open file in read only mode

---

[1]https://youtu.be/Pb01WoJRUtY

- "w" open a file for writing (and initializing a new file)
- "a" open a file for appending
- "rb", "wb", "ab" reading, writing, or appending in binary mode (Windows)

In practice, we often don't need to deal with the connection interface directly as many functions for reading and writing data just deal with it in the background.

For example, if one were to explicitly use connections to read a CSV file in to R, it might look like this,

```
> ## Create a connection to 'foo.txt'
> con <- file("foo.txt")
>
> ## Open connection to 'foo.txt' in read-only mode
> open(con, "r")
>
> ## Read from the connection
> data <- read.csv(con)
>
> ## Close the connection
> close(con)
```

which is the same as

```
> data <- read.csv("foo.txt")
```

In the background, `read.csv()` opens a connection to the file `foo.txt`, reads from it, and closes the connection when it's done.

The above example shows the basic approach to using connections. Connections must be opened, then the are read from or written to, and then they are closed.

9.2 Reading Lines of a Text File

Text files can be read line by line using the `readLines()` function. This function is useful for reading text files that may be unstructured or contain non-standard data.

```
> ## Open connection to gz-compressed text file
> con <- gzfile("words.gz")
> x <- readLines(con, 10)
> x
 [1] "1080"     "10-point" "10th"     "11-point" "12-point" "16-point"
 [7] "18-point" "1st"      "2"        "20-point"
```

For more structured text data like CSV files or tab-delimited files, there are other functions like read.csv() or read.table().

The above example used the gzfile() function which is used to create a connection to files compressed using the gzip algorithm. This approach is useful because it allows you to read from a file without having to uncompress the file first, which would be a waste of space and time.

There is a complementary function writeLines() that takes a character vector and writes each element of the vector one line at a time to a text file.

9.3 Reading From a URL Connection

The readLines() function can be useful for reading in lines of webpages. Since web pages are basically text files that are stored on a remote server, there is conceptually not much difference between a web page and a local text file. However, we need R to negotiate the communication between your computer and the web server. This is what the url() function can do for you, by creating a url connection to a web server.

This code might take time depending on your connection speed.

```
> ## Open a URL connection for reading
> con <- url("http://www.jhsph.edu", "r")
>
> ## Read the web page
> x <- readLines(con)
>
> ## Print out the first few lines
> head(x)
[1] "<!DOCTYPE html>"
[2] "<html lang=\"en\">"
[3] ""
[4] "<head>"
[5] "<meta charset=\"utf-8\" />"
[6] "<title>Johns Hopkins Bloomberg School of Public Health</title>"
```

While reading in a simple web page is sometimes useful, particularly if data are embedded in the web page somewhere. However, more commonly we can use URL connection to read in specific data files that are stored on web servers.

Using URL connections can be useful for producing a reproducible analysis, because the code essentially documents where the data came from and how they were obtained. This is approach is preferable to opening a web browser and downloading a dataset by hand. Of course, the code you write with connections may not be executable at a later date if things on the server side are changed or reorganized.

10. Subsetting R Objects

Watch a video of this section[1]

There are three operators that can be used to extract subsets of R objects.

- The [operator always returns an object of the same class as the original. It can be used to select multiple elements of an object
- The [[operator is used to extract elements of a list or a data frame. It can only be used to extract a single element and the class of the returned object will not necessarily be a list or data frame.
- The $ operator is used to extract elements of a list or data frame by literal name. Its semantics are similar to that of [[.

10.1 Subsetting a Vector

Vectors are basic objects in R and they can be subsetted using the [operator.

```
> x <- c("a", "b", "c", "c", "d", "a")
> x[1]     ## Extract the first element
[1] "a"
> x[2]     ## Extract the second element
[1] "b"
```

The [operator can be used to extract multiple elements of a vector by passing the operator an integer sequence. Here we extract the first four elements of the vector.

```
> x[1:4]
[1] "a" "b" "c" "c"
```

The sequence does not have to be in order; you can specify any arbitrary integer vector.

```
> x[c(1, 3, 4)]
[1] "a" "c" "c"
```

We can also pass a logical sequence to the [operator to extract elements of a vector that satisfy a given condition. For example, here we want the elements of x that come lexicographically *after* the letter "a".

---
[1]https://youtu.be/VfZUZGUgHqg

```
> u <- x > "a"
> u
[1] FALSE  TRUE  TRUE  TRUE  TRUE FALSE
> x[u]
[1] "b" "c" "c" "d"
```

Another, more compact, way to do this would be to skip the creation of a logical vector and just subset the vector directly with the logical expression.

```
> x[x > "a"]
[1] "b" "c" "c" "d"
```

10.2 Subsetting a Matrix

Watch a video of this section[2]

Matrices can be subsetted in the usual way with (i,j) type indices. Here, we create simple 2×3 matrix with the matrix function.

```
> x <- matrix(1:6, 2, 3)
> x
     [,1] [,2] [,3]
[1,]    1    3    5
[2,]    2    4    6
```

We can access the $(1, 2)$ or the $(2, 1)$ element of this matrix using the appropriate indices.

```
> x[1, 2]
[1] 3
> x[2, 1]
[1] 2
```

Indices can also be missing. This behavior is used to access entire rows or columns of a matrix.

```
> x[1, ]    ## Extract the first row
[1] 1 3 5
> x[, 2]    ## Extract the second column
[1] 3 4
```

Dropping matrix dimensions

By default, when a single element of a matrix is retrieved, it is returned as a vector of length 1 rather than a 1×1 matrix. Often, this is exactly what we want, but this behavior can be turned off by setting drop = FALSE.

[2]https://youtu.be/FzjXesh9tRw

```
> x <- matrix(1:6, 2, 3)
> x[1, 2]
[1] 3
> x[1, 2, drop = FALSE]
     [,1]
[1,]    3
```

Similarly, when we extract a single row or column of a matrix, R by default drops the dimension of length 1, so instead of getting a 1×3 matrix after extracting the first row, we get a vector of length 3. This behavior can similarly be turned off with the `drop = FALSE` option.

```
> x <- matrix(1:6, 2, 3)
> x[1, ]
[1] 1 3 5
> x[1, , drop = FALSE]
     [,1] [,2] [,3]
[1,]    1    3    5
```

Be careful of R's automatic dropping of dimensions. This is a feature that is often quite useful during interactive work, but can later come back to bite you when you are writing longer programs or functions.

10.3 Subsetting Lists

Watch a video of this section[3]

Lists in R can be subsetted using all three of the operators mentioned above, and all three are used for different purposes.

```
> x <- list(foo = 1:4, bar = 0.6)
> x
$foo
[1] 1 2 3 4

$bar
[1] 0.6
```

The `[[` operator can be used to extract *single* elements from a list. Here we extract the first element of the list.

---
[3]https://youtu.be/DStKguVpuDI

```
> x[[1]]
[1] 1 2 3 4
```

The [[operator can also use named indices so that you don't have to remember the exact ordering of every element of the list. You can also use the $ operator to extract elements by name.

```
> x[["bar"]]
[1] 0.6
> x$bar
[1] 0.6
```

Notice you don't need the quotes when you use the $ operator.

One thing that differentiates the [[operator from the $ is that the [[operator can be used with *computed* indices. The $ operator can only be used with literal names.

```
> x <- list(foo = 1:4, bar = 0.6, baz = "hello")
> name <- "foo"
>
> ## computed index for "foo"
> x[[name]]
[1] 1 2 3 4
>
> ## element "name" doesn't exist! (but no error here)
> x$name
NULL
>
> ## element "foo" does exist
> x$foo
[1] 1 2 3 4
```

10.4 Subsetting Nested Elements of a List

The [[operator can take an integer sequence if you want to extract a nested element of a list.

```
> x <- list(a = list(10, 12, 14), b = c(3.14, 2.81))
>
> ## Get the 3rd element of the 1st element
> x[[c(1, 3)]]
[1] 14
>
> ## Same as above
> x[[1]][[3]]
[1] 14
>
> ## 1st element of the 2nd element
> x[[c(2, 1)]]
[1] 3.14
```

10.5 Extracting Multiple Elements of a List

The [operator can be used to extract *multiple* elements from a list. For example, if you wanted to extract the first and third elements of a list, you would do the following

```
> x <- list(foo = 1:4, bar = 0.6, baz = "hello")
> x[c(1, 3)]
$foo
[1] 1 2 3 4

$baz
[1] "hello"
```

Note that x[c(1, 3)] is NOT the same as x[[c(1, 3)]].

Remember that the [operator always returns an object of the same class as the original. Since the original object was a list, the [operator returns a list. In the above code, we returned a list with two elements (the first and the third).

10.6 Partial Matching

Watch a video of this section[4]

Partial matching of names is allowed with [[and $. This is often very useful during interactive work if the object you're working with has very long element names. You can just abbreviate those names and R will figure out what element you're referring to.

---

[4]https://youtu.be/q3BNhHHVCu4

```
> x <- list(aardvark = 1:5)
> x$a
[1] 1 2 3 4 5
> x[["a"]]
NULL
> x[["a", exact = FALSE]]
[1] 1 2 3 4 5
```

In general, this is fine for interactive work, but you shouldn't resort to partial matching if you are writing longer scripts, functions, or programs. In those cases, you should refer to the full element name if possible. That way there's no ambiguity in your code.

10.7 Removing NA Values

Watch a video of this section[5]

A common task in data analysis is removing missing values (NAs).

```
> x <- c(1, 2, NA, 4, NA, 5)
> bad <- is.na(x)
> print(bad)
[1] FALSE FALSE  TRUE FALSE  TRUE FALSE
> x[!bad]
[1] 1 2 4 5
```

What if there are multiple R objects and you want to take the subset with no missing values in any of those objects?

```
> x <- c(1, 2, NA, 4, NA, 5)
> y <- c("a", "b", NA, "d", NA, "f")
> good <- complete.cases(x, y)
> good
[1]  TRUE  TRUE FALSE  TRUE FALSE  TRUE
> x[good]
[1] 1 2 4 5
> y[good]
[1] "a" "b" "d" "f"
```

You can use complete.cases on data frames too.

---
[5]https://youtu.be/TtJxmwXbwo0

```
> head(airquality)
  Ozone Solar.R Wind Temp Month Day
1    41     190  7.4   67     5   1
2    36     118  8.0   72     5   2
3    12     149 12.6   74     5   3
4    18     313 11.5   62     5   4
5    NA      NA 14.3   56     5   5
6    28      NA 14.9   66     5   6
> good <- complete.cases(airquality)
> head(airquality[good, ])
  Ozone Solar.R Wind Temp Month Day
1    41     190  7.4   67     5   1
2    36     118  8.0   72     5   2
3    12     149 12.6   74     5   3
4    18     313 11.5   62     5   4
7    23     299  8.6   65     5   7
8    19      99 13.8   59     5   8
```

11. Vectorized Operations

Watch a video of this chapter[1]

Many operations in R are *vectorized*, meaning that operations occur in parallel in certain R objects. This allows you to write code that is efficient, concise, and easier to read than in non-vectorized languages.

The simplest example is when adding two vectors together.

```
> x <- 1:4
> y <- 6:9
> z <- x + y
> z
[1]  7  9 11 13
```

Natural, right? Without vectorization, you'd have to do something like

```
z <- numeric(length(x))
for(i in seq_along(x)) {
      z[i] <- x[i] + y[i]
}
z
[1]  7  9 11 13
```

If you had to do that every time you wanted to add two vectors, your hands would get very tired from all the typing.

Another operation you can do in a vectorized manner is logical comparisons. So suppose you wanted to know which elements of a vector were greater than 2. You could do he following.

```
> x
[1] 1 2 3 4
> x > 2
[1] FALSE FALSE  TRUE  TRUE
```

Here are other vectorized logical operations.

---

[1] https://youtu.be/YH3qtw7mTyA

```
> x >= 2
[1] FALSE  TRUE  TRUE  TRUE
> x < 3
[1]  TRUE  TRUE FALSE FALSE
> y == 8
[1] FALSE FALSE  TRUE FALSE
```

Notice that these logical operations return a logical vector of TRUE and FALSE.

Of course, subtraction, multiplication and division are also vectorized.

```
> x - y
[1] -5 -5 -5 -5
> x * y
[1]  6 14 24 36
> x / y
[1] 0.1666667 0.2857143 0.3750000 0.4444444
```

11.1 Vectorized Matrix Operations

Matrix operations are also vectorized, making for nicly compact notation. This way, we can do element-by-element operations on matrices without having to loop over every element.

```
> x <- matrix(1:4, 2, 2)
> y <- matrix(rep(10, 4), 2, 2)
> 
> ## element-wise multiplication
> x * y
     [,1] [,2]
[1,]   10   30
[2,]   20   40
> 
> ## element-wise division
> x / y
     [,1] [,2]
[1,]  0.1  0.3
[2,]  0.2  0.4
> 
> ## true matrix multiplication
> x %*% y
     [,1] [,2]
[1,]   40   40
[2,]   60   60
```

12. Dates and Times

R has developed a special representation for dates and times. Dates are represented by the `Date` class and times are represented by the `POSIXct` or the `POSIXlt` class. Dates are stored internally as the number of days since 1970-01-01 while times are stored internally as the number of seconds since 1970-01-01.

It's not important to know the internal representation of dates and times in order to use them in R. I just thought those were fun facts.

12.1 Dates in R

Watch a video of this section[1]

Dates are represented by the `Date` class and can be coerced from a character string using the `as.Date()` function. This is a common way to end up with a `Date` object in R.

```
> ## Coerce a 'Date' object from character
> x <- as.Date("1970-01-01")
> x
[1] "1970-01-01"
```

You can see the internal representation of a `Date` object by using the `unclass()` function.

```
> unclass(x)
[1] 0
> unclass(as.Date("1970-01-02"))
[1] 1
```

12.2 Times in R

Watch a video of this section[2]

Times are represented by the `POSIXct` or the `POSIXlt` class. `POSIXct` is just a very large integer under the hood. It use a useful class when you want to store times in something like a data frame. `POSIXlt` is a list underneath and it stores a bunch of other useful information like the day of the week, day of the year, month, day of the month. This is useful when you need that kind of information.

There are a number of generic functions that work on dates and times to help you extract pieces of dates and/or times.

---
[1]https://youtu.be/opYexVgjwkE
[2]https://youtu.be/8HENCYXwZoU

- `weekdays`: give the day of the week
- `months`: give the month name
- `quarters`: give the quarter number ("Q1", "Q2", "Q3", or "Q4")

Times can be coerced from a character string using the `as.POSIXlt` or `as.POSIXct` function.

```
> x <- Sys.time()
> x
[1] "2016-04-20 08:29:15 EDT"
> class(x)      ## 'POSIXct' object
[1] "POSIXct" "POSIXt"
```

The `POSIXlt` object contains some useful metadata.

```
> p <- as.POSIXlt(x)
> names(unclass(p))
 [1] "sec"    "min"    "hour"   "mday"   "mon"    "year"   "wday"
 [8] "yday"   "isdst"  "zone"   "gmtoff"
> p$wday        ## day of the week
[1] 3
```

You can also use the `POSIXct` format.

```
> x <- Sys.time()
> x               ## Already in 'POSIXct' format
[1] "2016-04-20 08:29:15 EDT"
> unclass(x)      ## Internal representation
[1] 1461155355
> x$sec           ## Can't do this with 'POSIXct'!
Error in x$sec: $ operator is invalid for atomic vectors
> p <- as.POSIXlt(x)
> p$sec           ## That's better
[1] 15.31217
```

Finally, there is the `strptime()` function in case your dates are written in a different format. `strptime()` takes a character vector that has dates and times and converts them into to a `POSIXlt` object.

```
> datestring <- c("January 10, 2012 10:40", "December 9, 2011 9:10")
> x <- strptime(datestring, "%B %d, %Y %H:%M")
> x
[1] "2012-01-10 10:40:00 EST" "2011-12-09 09:10:00 EST"
> class(x)
[1] "POSIXlt" "POSIXt"
```

The weird-looking symbols that start with the % symbol are the formatting strings for dates and times. I can *never* remember the formatting strings. Check ?strptime for details. It's probably not worth memorizing this stuff.

12.3 Operations on Dates and Times

Watch a video of this section[3]

You can use mathematical operations on dates and times. Well, really just + and -. You can do comparisons too (i.e. ==, <=)

```
> x <- as.Date("2012-01-01")
> y <- strptime("9 Jan 2011 11:34:21", "%d %b %Y %H:%M:%S")
> x-y
Warning: Incompatible methods ("-.Date", "-.POSIXt") for "-"
Error in x - y: non-numeric argument to binary operator
> x <- as.POSIXlt(x)
> x-y
Time difference of 356.3095 days
```

The nice thing about the date/time classes is that they keep track of all the annoying things about dates and times, like leap years, leap seconds, daylight savings, and time zones.

Here's an example where a leap year gets involved.

```
> x <- as.Date("2012-03-01")
> y <- as.Date("2012-02-28")
> x-y
Time difference of 2 days
```

Here's an example where two different time zones are in play (unless you live in GMT timezone, in which case they will be the same!).

---
[3]https://youtu.be/vEmWJrpP1KM

```
> ## My local time zone
> x <- as.POSIXct("2012-10-25 01:00:00")
> y <- as.POSIXct("2012-10-25 06:00:00", tz = "GMT")
> y-x
Time difference of 1 hours
```

12.4 Summary

- Dates and times have special classes in R that allow for numerical and statistical calculations
- Dates use the Date class
- Times use the POSIXct and POSIXlt class
- Character strings can be coerced to Date/Time classes using the strptime function or the as.Date, as.POSIXlt, or as.POSIXct

13. Managing Data Frames with the `dplyr` package

Watch a video of this chapter[1]

13.1 Data Frames

The *data frame* is a key data structure in statistics and in R. The basic structure of a data frame is that there is one observation per row and each column represents a variable, a measure, feature, or characteristic of that observation. R has an internal implementation of data frames that is likely the one you will use most often. However, there are packages on CRAN that implement data frames via things like relational databases that allow you to operate on very very large data frames (but we won't discuss them here).

Given the importance of managing data frames, it's important that we have good tools for dealing with them. In previous chapters we have already discussed some tools like the `subset()` function and the use of `[` and `$` operators to extract subsets of data frames. However, other operations, like filtering, re-ordering, and collapsing, can often be tedious operations in R whose syntax is not very intuitive. The `dplyr` package is designed to mitigate a lot of these problems and to provide a highly optimized set of routines specifically for dealing with data frames.

13.2 The `dplyr` Package

The `dplyr` package was developed by Hadley Wickham of RStudio and is an optimized and distilled version of his `plyr` package. The `dplyr` package does not provide any "new" functionality to R per se, in the sense that everything `dplyr` does could already be done with base R, but it *greatly* simplifies existing functionality in R.

One important contribution of the `dplyr` package is that it provides a "grammar" (in particular, verbs) for data manipulation and for operating on data frames. With this grammar, you can sensibly communicate what it is that you are doing to a data frame that other people can understand (assuming they also know the grammar). This is useful because it provides an abstraction for data manipulation that previously did not exist. Another useful contribution is that the `dplyr` functions are **very** fast, as many key operations are coded in C++.

---

[1]https://youtu.be/aywFompr1F4

13.3 dplyr **Grammar**

Some of the key "verbs" provided by the dplyr package are

- select: return a subset of the columns of a data frame, using a flexible notation
- filter: extract a subset of rows from a data frame based on logical conditions
- arrange: reorder rows of a data frame
- rename: rename variables in a data frame
- mutate: add new variables/columns or transform existing variables
- summarise / summarize: generate summary statistics of different variables in the data frame, possibly within strata
- %>%: the "pipe" operator is used to connect multiple verb actions together into a pipeline

The dplyr package as a number of its own data types that it takes advantage of. For example, there is a handy print method that prevents you from printing a lot of data to the console. Most of the time, these additional data types are transparent to the user and do not need to be worried about.

Common dplyr **Function Properties**

All of the functions that we will discuss in this Chapter will have a few common characteristics. In particular,

1. The first argument is a data frame.
2. The subsequent arguments describe what to do with the data frame specified in the first argument, and you can refer to columns in the data frame directly without using the $ operator (just use the column names).
3. The return result of a function is a new data frame
4. Data frames must be properly formatted and annotated for this to all be useful. In particular, the data must be tidy[2]. In short, there should be one observation per row, and each column should represent a feature or characteristic of that observation.

13.4 Installing the dplyr **package**

The dplyr package can be installed from CRAN or from GitHub using the devtools package and the install_github() function. The GitHub repository will usually contain the latest updates to the package and the development version.

To install from CRAN, just run

---
[2]http://www.jstatsoft.org/v59/i10/paper

```
> install.packages("dplyr")
```

To install from GitHub you can run

```
> install_github("hadley/dplyr")
```

After installing the package it is important that you load it into your R session with the `library()` function.

```
> library(dplyr)

Attaching package: 'dplyr'
The following objects are masked from 'package:stats':

    filter, lag
The following objects are masked from 'package:base':

    intersect, setdiff, setequal, union
```

You may get some warnings when the package is loaded because there are functions in the `dplyr` package that have the same name as functions in other packages. For now you can ignore the warnings.

13.5 `select()`

For the examples in this chapter we will be using a dataset containing air pollution and temperature data for the city of Chicago[3] in the U.S. The dataset is available from my web site.

After unzipping the archive, you can load the data into R using the `readRDS()` function.

```
> chicago <- readRDS("chicago.rds")
```

You can see some basic characteristics of the dataset with the `dim()` and `str()` functions.

---

[3]http://www.biostat.jhsph.edu/~rpeng/leanpub/rprog/chicago_data.zip

```
> dim(chicago)
[1] 6940    8
> str(chicago)
'data.frame':    6940 obs. of  8 variables:
 $ city      : chr  "chic" "chic" "chic" "chic" ...
 $ tmpd      : num  31.5 33 33 29 32 40 34.5 29 26.5 32.5 ...
 $ dptp      : num  31.5 29.9 27.4 28.6 28.9 ...
 $ date      : Date, format: "1987-01-01" "1987-01-02" ...
 $ pm25tmean2: num  NA NA NA NA NA NA NA NA NA NA ...
 $ pm10tmean2: num  34 NA 34.2 47 NA ...
 $ o3tmean2  : num  4.25 3.3 3.33 4.38 4.75 ...
 $ no2tmean2 : num  20 23.2 23.8 30.4 30.3 ...
```

The `select()` function can be used to select columns of a data frame that you want to focus on. Often you'll have a large data frame containing "all" of the data, but any *given* analysis might only use a subset of variables or observations. The `select()` function allows you to get the few columns you might need.

Suppose we wanted to take the first 3 columns only. There are a few ways to do this. We could for example use numerical indices. But we can also use the names directly.

```
> names(chicago)[1:3]
[1] "city" "tmpd" "dptp"
> subset <- select(chicago, city:dptp)
> head(subset)
  city tmpd   dptp
1 chic 31.5 31.500
2 chic 33.0 29.875
3 chic 33.0 27.375
4 chic 29.0 28.625
5 chic 32.0 28.875
6 chic 40.0 35.125
```

Note that the : normally cannot be used with names or strings, but inside the `select()` function you can use it to specify a range of variable names.

You can also *omit* variables using the `select()` function by using the negative sign. With `select()` you can do

```
> select(chicago, -(city:dptp))
```

which indicates that we should include every variable *except* the variables `city` through `dptp`. The equivalent code in base R would be

```
> i <- match("city", names(chicago))
> j <- match("dptp", names(chicago))
> head(chicago[, -(i:j)])
```

Not super intuitive, right?

The `select()` function also allows a special syntax that allows you to specify variable names based on patterns. So, for example, if you wanted to keep every variable that ends with a "2", we could do

```
> subset <- select(chicago, ends_with("2"))
> str(subset)
'data.frame':    6940 obs. of  4 variables:
 $ pm25tmean2: num  NA NA NA NA NA NA NA NA NA NA ...
 $ pm10tmean2: num  34 NA 34.2 47 NA ...
 $ o3tmean2  : num  4.25 3.3 3.33 4.38 4.75 ...
 $ no2tmean2 : num  20 23.2 23.8 30.4 30.3 ...
```

Or if we wanted to keep every variable that starts with a "d", we could do

```
> subset <- select(chicago, starts_with("d"))
> str(subset)
'data.frame':    6940 obs. of  2 variables:
 $ dptp: num  31.5 29.9 27.4 28.6 28.9 ...
 $ date: Date, format: "1987-01-01" "1987-01-02" ...
```

You can also use more general regular expressions if necessary. See the help page (`?select`) for more details.

13.6 `filter()`

The `filter()` function is used to extract subsets of rows from a data frame. This function is similar to the existing `subset()` function in R but is quite a bit faster in my experience.

Suppose we wanted to extract the rows of the `chicago` data frame where the levels of PM2.5 are greater than 30 (which is a reasonably high level), we could do

```
> chic.f <- filter(chicago, pm25tmean2 > 30)
> str(chic.f)
'data.frame':        194 obs. of  8 variables:
 $ city       : chr  "chic" "chic" "chic" "chic" ...
 $ tmpd       : num  23 28 55 59 57 57 75 61 73 78 ...
 $ dptp       : num  21.9 25.8 51.3 53.7 52 56 65.8 59 60.3 67.1 ...
 $ date       : Date, format: "1998-01-17" "1998-01-23" ...
 $ pm25tmean2 : num  38.1 34 39.4 35.4 33.3 ...
 $ pm10tmean2 : num  32.5 38.7 34 28.5 35 ...
 $ o3tmean2   : num  3.18 1.75 10.79 14.3 20.66 ...
 $ no2tmean2  : num  25.3 29.4 25.3 31.4 26.8 ...
```

You can see that there are now only 194 rows in the data frame and the distribution of the pm25tmean2 values is.

```
> summary(chic.f$pm25tmean2)
   Min. 1st Qu.  Median    Mean 3rd Qu.    Max.
  30.05   32.12   35.04   36.63   39.53   61.50
```

We can place an arbitrarily complex logical sequence inside of filter(), so we could for example extract the rows where PM2.5 is greater than 30 *and* temperature is greater than 80 degrees Fahrenheit.

```
> chic.f <- filter(chicago, pm25tmean2 > 30 & tmpd > 80)
> select(chic.f, date, tmpd, pm25tmean2)
         date tmpd pm25tmean2
1  1998-08-23   81   39.60000
2  1998-09-06   81   31.50000
3  2001-07-20   82   32.30000
4  2001-08-01   84   43.70000
5  2001-08-08   85   38.83750
6  2001-08-09   84   38.20000
7  2002-06-20   82   33.00000
8  2002-06-23   82   42.50000
9  2002-07-08   81   33.10000
10 2002-07-18   82   38.85000
11 2003-06-25   82   33.90000
12 2003-07-04   84   32.90000
13 2005-06-24   86   31.85714
14 2005-06-27   82   51.53750
15 2005-06-28   85   31.20000
16 2005-07-17   84   32.70000
17 2005-08-03   84   37.90000
```

Now there are only 17 observations where both of those conditions are met.

13.7 `arrange()`

The `arrange()` function is used to reorder rows of a data frame according to one of the variables/columns. Reordering rows of a data frame (while preserving corresponding order of other columns) is normally a pain to do in R. The `arrange()` function simplifies the process quite a bit.

Here we can order the rows of the data frame by date, so that the first row is the earliest (oldest) observation and the last row is the latest (most recent) observation.

```
> chicago <- arrange(chicago, date)
```

We can now check the first few rows

```
> head(select(chicago, date, pm25tmean2), 3)
        date pm25tmean2
1 1987-01-01         NA
2 1987-01-02         NA
3 1987-01-03         NA
```

and the last few rows.

```
> tail(select(chicago, date, pm25tmean2), 3)
           date pm25tmean2
6938 2005-12-29    7.45000
6939 2005-12-30   15.05714
6940 2005-12-31   15.00000
```

Columns can be arranged in descending order too by useing the special `desc()` operator.

```
> chicago <- arrange(chicago, desc(date))
```

Looking at the first three and last three rows shows the dates in descending order.

```
> head(select(chicago, date, pm25tmean2), 3)
        date pm25tmean2
1 2005-12-31   15.00000
2 2005-12-30   15.05714
3 2005-12-29    7.45000
> tail(select(chicago, date, pm25tmean2), 3)
           date pm25tmean2
6938 1987-01-03         NA
6939 1987-01-02         NA
6940 1987-01-01         NA
```

13.8 rename()

Renaming a variable in a data frame in R is surprisingly hard to do! The rename() function is designed to make this process easier.

Here you can see the names of the first five variables in the chicago data frame.

```
> head(chicago[, 1:5], 3)
  city tmpd dptp       date pm25tmean2
1 chic   35 30.1 2005-12-31   15.00000
2 chic   36 31.0 2005-12-30   15.05714
3 chic   35 29.4 2005-12-29    7.45000
```

The dptp column is supposed to represent the dew point temperature adn the pm25tmean2 column provides the PM2.5 data. However, these names are pretty obscure or awkward and probably be renamed to something more sensible.

```
> chicago <- rename(chicago, dewpoint = dptp, pm25 = pm25tmean2)
> head(chicago[, 1:5], 3)
  city tmpd dewpoint       date     pm25
1 chic   35     30.1 2005-12-31 15.00000
2 chic   36     31.0 2005-12-30 15.05714
3 chic   35     29.4 2005-12-29  7.45000
```

The syntax inside the rename() function is to have the new name on the left-hand side of the = sign and the old name on the right-hand side.

I leave it as an exercise for the reader to figure how you do this in base R without dplyr.

13.9 mutate()

The mutate() function exists to compute transformations of variables in a data frame. Often, you want to create new variables that are derived from existing variables and mutate() provides a clean interface for doing that.

For example, with air pollution data, we often want to *detrend* the data by subtracting the mean from the data. That way we can look at whether a given day's air pollution level is higher than or less than average (as opposed to looking at its absolute level).

Here we create a pm25detrend variable that subtracts the mean from the pm25 variable.

```
> chicago <- mutate(chicago, pm25detrend = pm25 - mean(pm25, na.rm = TRUE))
> head(chicago)
  city tmpd dewpoint       date     pm25 pm10tmean2 o3tmean2 no2tmean2
1 chic   35     30.1 2005-12-31 15.00000       23.5  2.531250  13.25000
2 chic   36     31.0 2005-12-30 15.05714       19.2  3.034420  22.80556
3 chic   35     29.4 2005-12-29  7.45000       23.5  6.794837  19.97222
4 chic   37     34.5 2005-12-28 17.75000       27.5  3.260417  19.28563
5 chic   40     33.6 2005-12-27 23.56000       27.0  4.468750  23.50000
6 chic   35     29.6 2005-12-26  8.40000        8.5 14.041667  16.81944
  pm25detrend
1   -1.230958
2   -1.173815
3   -8.780958
4    1.519042
5    7.329042
6   -7.830958
```

There is also the related transmute() function, which does the same thing as mutate() but then *drops all non-transformed variables*.

Here we detrend the PM10 and ozone (O3) variables.

```
> head(transmute(chicago,
+                pm10detrend = pm10tmean2 - mean(pm10tmean2, na.rm = TRUE),
+                o3detrend = o3tmean2 - mean(o3tmean2, na.rm = TRUE)))
  pm10detrend  o3detrend
1  -10.395206 -16.904263
2  -14.695206 -16.401093
3  -10.395206 -12.640676
4   -6.395206 -16.175096
5   -6.895206 -14.966763
6  -25.395206  -5.393846
```

Note that there are only two columns in the transmuted data frame.

13.10 group_by()

The group_by() function is used to generate summary statistics from the data frame within strata defined by a variable. For example, in this air pollution dataset, you might want to know what the average annual level of PM2.5 is. So the stratum is the year, and that is something we can derive from the date variable. In conjunction with the group_by() function we often use the summarize() function (or summarise() for some parts of the world).

The general operation here is a combination of splitting a data frame into separate pieces defined by a variable or group of variables (group_by()), and then applying a summary function across those subsets (summarize()).

First, we can create a year varible using as.POSIXlt().

```
> chicago <- mutate(chicago, year = as.POSIXlt(date)$year + 1900)
```

Now we can create a separate data frame that splits the original data frame by year.

```
> years <- group_by(chicago, year)
```

Finally, we compute summary statistics for each year in the data frame with the summarize() function.

```
> summarize(years, pm25 = mean(pm25, na.rm = TRUE),
+           o3 = max(o3tmean2, na.rm = TRUE),
+           no2 = median(no2tmean2, na.rm = TRUE))
Source: local data frame [19 x 4]

      year     pm25       o3      no2
     (dbl)    (dbl)    (dbl)    (dbl)
1     1987      NaN 62.96966 23.49369
2     1988      NaN 61.67708 24.52296
3     1989      NaN 59.72727 26.14062
4     1990      NaN 52.22917 22.59583
5     1991      NaN 63.10417 21.38194
6     1992      NaN 50.82870 24.78921
7     1993      NaN 44.30093 25.76993
8     1994      NaN 52.17844 28.47500
9     1995      NaN 66.58750 27.26042
10    1996      NaN 58.39583 26.38715
11    1997      NaN 56.54167 25.48143
12    1998 18.26467 50.66250 24.58649
13    1999 18.49646 57.48864 24.66667
14    2000 16.93806 55.76103 23.46082
```

```
15  2001 16.92632 51.81984 25.06522
16  2002 15.27335 54.88043 22.73750
17  2003 15.23183 56.16608 24.62500
18  2004 14.62864 44.48240 23.39130
19  2005 16.18556 58.84126 22.62387
```

summarize() returns a data frame with year as the first column, and then the annual averages of pm25, o3, and no2.

In a slightly more complicated example, we might want to know what are the average levels of ozone (o3) and nitrogen dioxide (no2) within quintiles of pm25. A slicker way to do this would be through a regression model, but we can actually do this quickly with group_by() and summarize().

First, we can create a categorical variable of pm25 divided into quintiles.

```
> qq <- quantile(chicago$pm25, seq(0, 1, 0.2), na.rm = TRUE)
> chicago <- mutate(chicago, pm25.quint = cut(pm25, qq))
```

Now we can group the data frame by the pm25.quint variable.

```
> quint <- group_by(chicago, pm25.quint)
```

Finally, we can compute the mean of o3 and no2 within quintiles of pm25.

```
> summarize(quint, o3 = mean(o3tmean2, na.rm = TRUE),
+           no2 = mean(no2tmean2, na.rm = TRUE))
Source: local data frame [6 x 3]

  pm25.quint       o3       no2
      (fctr)    (dbl)     (dbl)
1  (1.7,8.7] 21.66401  17.99129
2 (8.7,12.4] 20.38248  22.13004
3 (12.4,16.7] 20.66160 24.35708
4 (16.7,22.6] 19.88122 27.27132
5 (22.6,61.5] 20.31775 29.64427
6         NA 18.79044  25.77585
```

From the table, it seems there isn't a strong relationship between pm25 and o3, but there appears to be a positive correlation between pm25 and no2. More sophisticated statistical modeling can help to provide precise answers to these questions, but a simple application of dplyr functions can often get you most of the way there.

13.11 %>%

The pipeline operater %>% is very handy for stringing together multiple dplyr functions in a sequence of operations. Notice above that every time we wanted to apply more than one function, the sequence gets buried in a sequence of nested function calls that is difficult to read, i.e.

```
> third(second(first(x)))
```

This nesting is not a natural way to think about a sequence of operations. The %>% operator allows you to string operations in a left-to-right fashion, i.e.

```
> first(x) %>% second %>% third
```

Take the example that we just did in the last section where we computed the mean of o3 and no2 within quintiles of pm25. There we had to

1. create a new variable pm25.quint
2. split the data frame by that new variable
3. compute the mean of o3 and no2 in the sub-groups defined by pm25.quint

That can be done with the following sequence in a single R expression.

```
> mutate(chicago, pm25.quint = cut(pm25, qq)) %>%
+         group_by(pm25.quint) %>%
+         summarize(o3 = mean(o3tmean2, na.rm = TRUE),
+                   no2 = mean(no2tmean2, na.rm = TRUE))
Source: local data frame [6 x 3]

  pm25.quint        o3       no2
      (fctr)     (dbl)     (dbl)
1  (1.7,8.7]  21.66401  17.99129
2  (8.7,12.4] 20.38248  22.13004
3 (12.4,16.7] 20.66160  24.35708
4 (16.7,22.6] 19.88122  27.27132
5 (22.6,61.5] 20.31775  29.64427
6          NA 18.79044  25.77585
```

This way we don't have to create a set of temporary variables along the way or create a massive nested sequence of function calls.

Notice in the above code that I pass the chicago data frame to the first call to mutate(), but then afterwards I do not have to pass the first argument to group_by() or summarize(). Once you travel down the pipeline with %>%, the first argument is taken to be the output of the previous element in the pipeline.

Another example might be computing the average pollutant level by month. This could be useful to see if there are any seasonal trends in the data.

```
> mutate(chicago, month = as.POSIXlt(date)$mon + 1) %>%
+         group_by(month) %>%
+         summarize(pm25 = mean(pm25, na.rm = TRUE),
+                   o3 = max(o3tmean2, na.rm = TRUE),
+                   no2 = median(no2tmean2, na.rm = TRUE))
Source: local data frame [12 x 4]

   month     pm25       o3      no2
   (dbl)    (dbl)    (dbl)    (dbl)
1      1 17.76996 28.22222 25.35417
2      2 20.37513 37.37500 26.78034
3      3 17.40818 39.05000 26.76984
4      4 13.85879 47.94907 25.03125
5      5 14.07420 52.75000 24.22222
6      6 15.86461 66.58750 25.01140
7      7 16.57087 59.54167 22.38442
8      8 16.93380 53.96701 22.98333
9      9 15.91279 57.48864 24.47917
10    10 14.23557 47.09275 24.15217
11    11 15.15794 29.45833 23.56537
12    12 17.52221 27.70833 24.45773
```

Here we can see that o3 tends to be low in the winter months and high in the summer while no2 is higher in the winter and lower in the summer.

13.12 Summary

The dplyr package provides a concise set of operations for managing data frames. With these functions we can do a number of complex operations in just a few lines of code. In particular, we can often conduct the beginnings of an exploratory analysis with the powerful combination of group_by() and summarize().

Once you learn the dplyr grammar there are a few additional benefits

- dplyr can work with other data frame "backends" such as SQL databases. There is an SQL interface for relational databases via the DBI package
- dplyr can be integrated with the data.table package for large fast tables

The dplyr package is handy way to both simplify and speed up your data frame management code. It's rare that you get such a combination at the same time!

14. Control Structures

Watch a video of this section[1]

Control structures in R allow you to control the flow of execution of a series of R expressions. Basically, control structures allow you to put some "logic" into your R code, rather than just always executing the same R code every time. Control structures allow you to respond to inputs or to features of the data and execute different R expressions accordingly.

Commonly used control structures are

- `if` and `else`: testing a condition and acting on it
- `for`: execute a loop a fixed number of times
- `while`: execute a loop *while* a condition is true
- `repeat`: execute an infinite loop (must `break` out of it to stop)
- `break`: break the execution of a loop
- `next`: skip an interation of a loop

Most control structures are not used in interactive sessions, but rather when writing functions or longer expresisons. However, these constructs do not have to be used in functions and it's a good idea to become familiar with them before we delve into functions.

14.1 `if-else`

Watch a video of this section[2]

The `if-else` combination is probably the most commonly used control structure in R (or perhaps any language). This structure allows you to test a condition and act on it depending on whether it's true or false.

For starters, you can just use the `if` statement.

---

[1]https://youtu.be/BPNLjUDZ8_o
[2]https://youtu.be/ZaBtJPYYGwg

```
if(<condition>) {
        ## do something
}
## Continue with rest of code
```

The above code does nothing if the condition is false. If you have an action you want to execute when the condition is false, then you need an `else` clause.

```
if(<condition>) {
        ## do something
}
else {
        ## do something else
}
```

You can have a series of tests by following the initial `if` with any number of `else if`s.

```
if(<condition1>) {
        ## do something
} else if(<condition2>) {
        ## do something different
} else {
        ## do something different
}
```

Here is an example of a valid if/else structure.

```
## Generate a uniform random number
x <- runif(1, 0, 10)
if(x > 3) {
        y <- 10
} else {
        y <- 0
}
```

The value of `y` is set depending on whether `x > 3` or not. This expression can also be written a different, but equivalent, way in R.

```
y <- if(x > 3) {
        10
} else {
        0
}
```

Neither way of writing this expression is more correct than the other. Which one you use will depend on your preference and perhaps those of the team you may be working with.

Of course, the `else` clause is not necessary. You could have a series of if clauses that always get executed if their respective conditions are true.

```
if(<condition1>) {

}

if(<condition2>) {

}
```

14.2 for Loops

Watch a video of this section[3]

For loops are pretty much the only looping construct that you will need in R. While you may occasionally find a need for other types of loops, in my experience doing data analysis, I've found very few situations where a for loop wasn't sufficient.

In R, for loops take an interator variable and assign it successive values from a sequence or vector. For loops are most commonly used for iterating over the elements of an object (list, vector, etc.)

```
> for(i in 1:10) {
+         print(i)
+ }
[1] 1
[1] 2
[1] 3
[1] 4
[1] 5
[1] 6
[1] 7
[1] 8
[1] 9
[1] 10
```

---

[3]https://youtu.be/FbT1dGXCCxU

This loop takes the i variable and in each iteration of the loop gives it values 1, 2, 3, ..., 10, executes the code within the curly braces, and then the loop exits.

The following three loops all have the same behavior.

```
> x <- c("a", "b", "c", "d")
>
> for(i in 1:4) {
+         ## Print out each element of 'x'
+         print(x[i])
+ }
[1] "a"
[1] "b"
[1] "c"
[1] "d"
```

The seq_along() function is commonly used in conjunction with for loops in order to generate an integer sequence based on the length of an object (in this case, the object x).

```
> ## Generate a sequence based on length of 'x'
> for(i in seq_along(x)) {
+         print(x[i])
+ }
[1] "a"
[1] "b"
[1] "c"
[1] "d"
```

It is not necessary to use an index-type variable.

```
> for(letter in x) {
+         print(letter)
+ }
[1] "a"
[1] "b"
[1] "c"
[1] "d"
```

For one line loops, the curly braces are not strictly necessary.

```
> for(i in 1:4) print(x[i])
[1] "a"
[1] "b"
[1] "c"
[1] "d"
```

However, I like to use curly braces even for one-line loops, because that way if you decide to expand the loop to multiple lines, you won't be burned because you forgot to add curly braces (and you *will* be burned by this).

14.3 Nested `for` loops

`for` loops can be nested inside of each other.

```
x <- matrix(1:6, 2, 3)

for(i in seq_len(nrow(x))) {
        for(j in seq_len(ncol(x))) {
                print(x[i, j])
        }
}
```

Nested loops are commonly needed for multidimensional or hierarchical data structures (e.g. matrices, lists). Be careful with nesting though. Nesting beyond 2 to 3 levels often makes it difficult to read/understand the code. If you find yourself in need of a large number of nested loops, you may want to break up the loops by using functions (discussed later).

14.4 `while` Loops

Watch a video of this section[4]

While loops begin by testing a condition. If it is true, then they execute the loop body. Once the loop body is executed, the condition is tested again, and so forth, until the condition is false, after which the loop exits.

---

[4]https://youtu.be/VqrS1Wghq1c

```
> count <- 0
> while(count < 10) {
+         print(count)
+         count <- count + 1
+ }
[1] 0
[1] 1
[1] 2
[1] 3
[1] 4
[1] 5
[1] 6
[1] 7
[1] 8
[1] 9
```

While loops can potentially result in infinite loops if not written properly. Use with care!

Sometimes there will be more than one condition in the test.

```
> z <- 5
> set.seed(1)
>
> while(z >= 3 && z <= 10) {
+         coin <- rbinom(1, 1, 0.5)
+
+         if(coin == 1) {  ## random walk
+                 z <- z + 1
+         } else {
+                 z <- z - 1
+         }
+ }
> print(z)
[1] 2
```

Conditions are always evaluated from left to right. For example, in the above code, if z were less than 3, the second test would not have been evaluated.

14.5 repeat Loops

Watch a video of this section[5]

---
[5]https://youtu.be/SajmdYr30SY

repeat initiates an infinite loop right from the start. These are not commonly used in statistical or data analysis applications but they do have their uses. The only way to exit a repeat loop is to call break.

One possible paradigm might be in an iterative algorith where you may be searching for a solution and you don't want to stop until you're close enough to the solution. In this kind of situation, you often don't know in advance how many iterations it's going to take to get "close enough" to the solution.

```
x0 <- 1
tol <- 1e-8

repeat {
        x1 <- computeEstimate()

        if(abs(x1 - x0) < tol) {   ## Close enough?
                break
        } else {
                x0 <- x1
        }
}
```

Note that the above code will not run if the computeEstimate() function is not defined (I just made it up for the purposes of this demonstration).

The loop above is a bit dangerous because there's no guarantee it will stop. You could get in a situation where the values of x0 and x1 oscillate back and forth and never converge. Better to set a hard limit on the number of iterations by using a for loop and then report whether convergence was achieved or not.

14.6 next, break

next is used to skip an iteration of a loop.

```
for(i in 1:100) {
        if(i <= 20) {
                ## Skip the first 20 iterations
                next
        }
        ## Do something here
}
```

break is used to exit a loop immediately, regardless of what iteration the loop may be on.

```
for(i in 1:100) {
        print(i)

        if(i > 20) {
                ## Stop loop after 20 iterations
                break
        }
}
```

14.7 Summary

- Control structures like if, while, and for allow you to control the flow of an R program
- Infinite loops should generally be avoided, even if (you believe) they are theoretically correct.
- Control structures mentiond here are primarily useful for writing programs; for command-line interactive work, the "apply" functions are more useful.

15. Functions

Writing functions is a core activity of an R programmer. It represents the key step of the transition from a mere "user" to a developer who creates new functionality for R. Functions are often used to encapsulate a sequence of expressions that need to be executed numerous times, perhaps under slightly different conditions. Functions are also often written when code must be shared with others or the public.

The writing of a function allows a developer to create an interface to the code, that is explicitly specified with a set of parameters. This interface provides an abstraction of the code to potential users. This abstraction simplifies the users' lives because it relieves them from having to know every detail of how the code operates. In addition, the creation of an interface allows the developer to communicate to the user the aspects of the code that are important or are most relevant.

15.1 Functions in R

Functions in R are "first class objects", which means that they can be treated much like any other R object. Importantly,

- Functions can be passed as arguments to other functions. This is very handy for the various apply funtions, like `lapply()` and `sapply()`.
- Functions can be nested, so that you can define a function inside of another function

If you're familiar with common language like C, these features might appear a bit strange. However, they are really important in R and can be useful for data analysis.

15.2 Your First Function

Functions are defined using the `function()` directive and are stored as R objects just like anything else. In particular, they are R objects of class "function".

Here's a simple function that takes no arguments and does nothing.

```
> f <- function() {
+         ## This is an empty function
+ }
> ## Functions have their own class
> class(f)
[1] "function"
> ## Execute this function
> f()
NULL
```

Not very interesting, but it's a start. The next thing we can do is create a function that actually has a non-trivial *function body*.

```
> f <- function() {
+         cat("Hello, world!\n")
+ }
> f()
Hello, world!
```

The last aspect of a basic function is the *function arguments*. These are the options that you can specify to the user that the user may explicity set. For this basic function, we can add an argument that determines how many times "Hello, world!" is printed to the console.

```
> f <- function(num) {
+         for(i in seq_len(num)) {
+                 cat("Hello, world!\n")
+         }
+ }
> f(3)
Hello, world!
Hello, world!
Hello, world!
```

Obviously, we could have just cut-and-pasted the cat("Hello, world!\n") code three times to achieve the same effect, but then we wouldn't be programming, would we? Also, it would be un-neighborly of you to give your code to someone else and force them to cut-and-paste the code however many times the need to see "Hello, world!".

> In general, if you find yourself doing a lot of cutting and pasting, that's usually a good sign that you might need to write a function.

Finally, the function above doesn't *return* anything. It just prints "Hello, world!" to the console num number of times and then exits. But often it is useful if a function returns something that perhaps can be fed into another section of code.

This next function returns the total number of characters printed to the console.

```
> f <- function(num) {
+         hello <- "Hello, world!\n"
+         for(i in seq_len(num)) {
+                 cat(hello)
+         }
+         chars <- nchar(hello) * num
+         chars
+ }
> meaningoflife <- f(3)
Hello, world!
Hello, world!
Hello, world!
> print(meaningoflife)
[1] 42
```

In the above function, we didn't have to indicate anything special in order for the function to return the number of characters. In R, the return value of a function is always the very last expression that is evaluated. Because the chars variable is the last expression that is evaluated in this function, that becomes the return value of the function.

Note that there is a return() function that can be used to return an explicity value from a function, but it is rarely used in R (we will discuss it a bit later in this chapter).

Finally, in the above function, the user must specify the value of the argument num. If it is not specified by the user, R will throw an error.

```
> f()
Error in f(): argument "num" is missing, with no default
```

We can modify this behavior by setting a *default value* for the argument num. Any function argument can have a default value, if you wish to specify it. Sometimes, argument values are rarely modified (except in special cases) and it makes sense to set a default value for that argument. This relieves the user from having to specify the value of that argument every single time the function is called.

Here, for example, we could set the default value for num to be 1, so that if the function is called without the num argument being explicitly specified, then it will print "Hello, world!" to the console once.

```
> f <- function(num = 1) {
+         hello <- "Hello, world!\n"
+         for(i in seq_len(num)) {
+                 cat(hello)
+         }
+         chars <- nchar(hello) * num
+         chars
+ }
> f()    ## Use default value for 'num'
Hello, world!
[1] 14
> f(2)   ## Use user-specified value
Hello, world!
Hello, world!
[1] 28
```

Remember that the function still returns the number of characters printed to the console.

At this point, we have written a function that

- has one *formal argument* named num with a *default value* of 1. The *formal arguments* are the arguments included in the function definition. The formals() function returns a list of all the formal arguments of a function
- prints the message "Hello, world!" to the console a number of times indicated by the argument num
- *returns* the number of characters printed to the console

Functions have *named arguments* which can optionally have default values. Because all function arguments have names, they can be specified using their name.

```
> f(num = 2)
Hello, world!
Hello, world!
[1] 28
```

Specifying an argument by its name is sometimes useful if a function has many arguments and it may not always be clear which argument is being specified. Here, our function only has one argument so there's no confusion.

15.3 Argument Matching

Calling an R function with arguments can be done in a variety of ways. This may be confusing at first, but it's really handing when doing interactive work at the command line. R functions arguments can be matched *positionally* or by name. Positional matching just means that R assigns the first value to the first argument, the second value to second argument, etc. So in the following call to rnorm()

```
> str(rnorm)
function (n, mean = 0, sd = 1)
> mydata <- rnorm(100, 2, 1)          ## Generate some data
```

100 is assigned to the n argument, 2 is assigned to the mean argument, and 1 is assigned to the sd argument, all by positional matching.

The following calls to the sd() function (which computes the empirical standard deviation of a vector of numbers) are all equivalent. Note that sd() has two arguments: x indicates the vector of numbers and na.rm is a logical indicating whether missing values should be removed or not.

```
> ## Positional match first argument, default for 'na.rm'
> sd(mydata)
[1] 1.016235
> ## Specify 'x' argument by name, default for 'na.rm'
> sd(x = mydata)
[1] 1.016235
> ## Specify both arguments by name
> sd(x = mydata, na.rm = FALSE)
[1] 1.016235
```

When specifying the function arguments by name, it doesn't matter in what order you specify them. In the example below, we specify the na.rm argument first, followed by x, even though x is the first argument defined in the function definition.

```
> ## Specify both arguments by name
> sd(na.rm = FALSE, x = mydata)
[1] 1.016235
```

You can mix positional matching with matching by name. When an argument is matched by name, it is "taken out" of the argument list and the remaining unnamed arguments are matched in the order that they are listed in the function definition.

```
> sd(na.rm = FALSE, mydata)
[1] 1.016235
```

Here, the mydata object is assigned to the x argument, because it's the only argument not yet specified.

Below is the argument list for the lm() function, which fits linear models to a dataset.

```
> args(lm)
function (formula, data, subset, weights, na.action, method = "qr",
    model = TRUE, x = FALSE, y = FALSE, qr = TRUE, singular.ok = TRUE,
    contrasts = NULL, offset, ...)
NULL
```

The following two calls are equivalent.

```
lm(data = mydata, y ~ x, model = FALSE, 1:100)
lm(y ~ x, mydata, 1:100, model = FALSE)
```

Even though it's legal, I don't recommend messing around with the order of the arguments too much, since it can lead to some confusion.

Most of the time, named arguments are useful on the command line when you have a long argument list and you want to use the defaults for everything except for an argument near the end of the list. Named arguments also help if you can remember the name of the argument and not its position on the argument list. For example, plotting functions often have a lot of options to allow for customization, but this makes it difficult to remember exactly the position of every argument on the argument list.

Function arguments can also be *partially* matched, which is useful for interactive work. The order of operations when given an argument is

1. Check for exact match for a named argument
2. Check for a partial match
3. Check for a positional match

Partial matching should be avoided when writing longer code or programs, because it may lead to confusion if someone is reading the code. However, partial matching is very useful when calling functions interactively that have very long argument names.

In addition to not specifying a default value, you can also set an argument value to NULL.

```
f <- function(a, b = 1, c = 2, d = NULL) {

}
```

You can check to see whether an R object is NULL with the is.null() function. It is sometimes useful to allow an argument to take the NULL value, which might indicate that the function should take some specific action.

15.4 Lazy Evaluation

Arguments to functions are evaluated *lazily*, so they are evaluated only as needed in the body of the function.

In this example, the function f( ) has two arguments: a and b.

```
> f <- function(a, b) {
+       a^2
+ }
> f(2)
[1] 4
```

This function never actually uses the argument b, so calling f(2) will not produce an error because the 2 gets positionally matched to a. This behavior can be good or bad. It's common to write a function that doesn't use an argument and not notice it simply because R never throws an error.

This example also shows lazy evaluation at work, but does eventually result in an error.

```
> f <- function(a, b) {
+       print(a)
+       print(b)
+ }
> f(45)
[1] 45
Error in print(b): argument "b" is missing, with no default
```

Notice that "45" got printed first before the error was triggered. This is because b did not have to be evaluated until after print(a). Once the function tried to evaluate print(b) the function had to throw an error.

15.5 The ... Argument

There is a special argument in R known as the ... argument, which indicate a variable number of arguments that are usually passed on to other functions. The ... argument is often used when extending another function and you don't want to copy the entire argument list of the original function

For example, a custom plotting function may want to make use of the default plot( ) function along with its entire argument list. The function below changes the default for the type argument to the value type = "l" (the original default was type = "p").

```
myplot <- function(x, y, type = "l", ...) {
        plot(x, y, type = type, ...)      ## Pass '...' to 'plot' function
}
```

Generic functions use ... so that extra arguments can be passed to methods.

```
> mean
function (x, ...)
UseMethod("mean")
<bytecode: 0x7fe0699a4ae0>
<environment: namespace:base>
```

The ... argument is necessary when the number of arguments passed to the function cannot be known in advance. This is clear in functions like paste() and cat().

```
> args(paste)
function (..., sep = " ", collapse = NULL)
NULL
> args(cat)
function (..., file = "", sep = " ", fill = FALSE, labels = NULL,
    append = FALSE)
NULL
```

Because both paste() and cat() print out text to the console by combining multiple character vectors together, it is impossible for those functions to know in advance how many character vectors will be passed to the function by the user. So the first argument to either function is ....

15.6 Arguments Coming After the ... Argument

One catch with ... is that any arguments that appear *after* ... on the argument list must be named explicitly and cannot be partially matched or matched positionally.

Take a look at the arguments to the paste() function.

```
> args(paste)
function (..., sep = " ", collapse = NULL)
NULL
```

With the paste() function, the arguments sep and collapse must be named explicitly and in full if the default values are not going to be used.

Here I specify that I want "a" and "b" to be pasted together and separated by a colon.

```
> paste("a", "b", sep = ":")
[1] "a:b"
```

If I don't specify the `sep` argument in full and attempt to rely on partial matching, I don't get the expected result.

```
> paste("a", "b", se = ":")
[1] "a b :"
```

15.7 Summary

- Functions can be defined using the `function()` directive and are assigned to R objects just like any other R object
- Functions have can be defined with named arguments; these function arguments can have default values
- Functions arguments can be specified by name or by position in the argument list
- Functions always return the last expression evaluated in the function body
- A variable number of arguments can be specified using the special . . . argument in a function definition.

16. Scoping Rules of R

16.1 A Diversion on Binding Values to Symbol

Watch a video of this section[1]

How does R know which value to assign to which symbol? When I type

```
> lm <- function(x) { x * x }
> lm
function(x) { x * x }
```

how does R know what value to assign to the symbol `lm`? Why doesn't it give it the value of `lm` that is in the `stats` package?

When R tries to bind a value to a symbol, it searches through a series of `environments` to find the appropriate value. When you are working on the command line and need to retrieve the value of an R object, the order in which things occur is roughly

1. Search the global environment (i.e. your workspace) for a symbol name matching the one requested.
2. Search the namespaces of each of the packages on the search list

The search list can be found by using the `search()` function.

```
> search()
[1] ".GlobalEnv"        "package:knitr"     "package:stats"
[4] "package:graphics"  "package:grDevices" "package:utils"
[7] "package:datasets"  "Autoloads"         "package:base"
```

The *global environment* or the user's workspace is always the first element of the search list and the `base` package is always the last. For better or for worse, the order of the packages on the search list matters, particularly if there are multiple objects with the same name in different packages.

Users can configure which packages get loaded on startup so if you are writing a function (or a package), you cannot assume that there will be a set list of packages available in a given order. When a user loads a package with `library()` the namespace of that package gets put in position 2 of the search list (by default) and everything else gets shifted down the list.

Note that R has separate namespaces for functions and non-functions so it's possible to have an object named `c` and a function named `c()`.

---

[1]https://youtu.be/ujdm01Vsrmo

16.2 Scoping Rules

The scoping rules for R are the main feature that make it different from the original S language (in case you care about that). This may seem like an esoteric aspect of R, but it's one of its more interesting and useful features.

The scoping rules of a language determine how a value is associated with a *free variable* in a function. R uses *lexical scoping*[2] or *static scoping*. An alternative to lexical scoping is *dynamic scoping* which is implemented by some languages. Lexical scoping turns out to be particularly useful for simplifying statistical computations

Related to the scoping rules is how R uses the *search list* to bind a value to a symbol

Consider the following function.

```
> f <- function(x, y) {
+         x^2 + y / z
+ }
```

This function has 2 formal arguments x and y. In the body of the function there is another symbol z. In this case z is called a *free variable*.

The scoping rules of a language determine how values are assigned to free variables. Free variables are not formal arguments and are not local variables (assigned insided the function body).

Lexical scoping in R means that

> *the values of free variables are searched for in the environment in which the function was defined.*

Okay then, what is an environment?

An *environment* is a collection of (symbol, value) pairs, i.e. x is a symbol and 3.14 might be its value. Every environment has a parent environment and it is possible for an environment to have multiple "children". The only environment without a parent is the *empty environment.*

A function, together with an environment, makes up what is called a *closure* or *function closure*. Most of the time we don't need to think too much about a function and its associated environment (making up the closure), but occasionally, this setup can be very useful. The function closure model can be used to create functions that "carry around" data with them.

How do we associate a value to a free variable? There is a search process that occurs that goes as follows:

---

[2]http://en.wikipedia.org/wiki/Scope_(computer_science)#Lexical_scope_vs._dynamic_scope

- If the value of a symbol is not found in the environment in which a function was defined, then the search is continued in the *parent environment*.
- The search continues down the sequence of parent environments until we hit the *top-level environment*; this usually the global environment (workspace) or the namespace of a package.
- After the top-level environment, the search continues down the search list until we hit the *empty environment*.

If a value for a given symbol cannot be found once the empty environment is arrived at, then an error is thrown.

One implication of this search process is that it can be affected by the number of packages you have attached to the search list. The more packages you have attached, the more symbols R has to sort through in order to assign a value. That said, you'd have to have a pretty large number of packages attached in order to notice a real difference in performance.

16.3 Lexical Scoping: Why Does It Matter?

Watch a video of this section[3]

Typically, a function is defined in the global environment, so that the values of free variables are just found in the user's workspace. This behavior is logical for most people and is usually the "right thing" to do. However, in R you can have functions defined *inside other functions* (languages like C don't let you do this). Now things get interesting—in this case the environment in which a function is defined is the body of another function!

Here is an example of a function that returns another function as its return value. Remember, in R functions are treated like any other object and so this is perfectly valid.

```
> make.power <- function(n) {
+         pow <- function(x) {
+                 x^n
+         }
+         pow
+ }
```

The make.power() function is a kind of "constructor function" that can be used to construct other functions.

---
[3]https://youtu.be/yYzPhtF6--A

```
> cube <- make.power(3)
> square <- make.power(2)
> cube(3)
[1] 27
> square(3)
[1] 9
```

Let's take a look at the cube() function's code.

```
> cube
function(x) {
            x^n
    }
<environment: 0x7fbe6300c358>
```

Notice that cube() has a free variable n. What is the value of n here? Well, its value is taken from the environment where the function was defined. When I defined the cube() function it was when I called make.power(3), so the value of n at that time was 3.

We can explore the environment of a function to see what objects are there and their values.

```
> ls(environment(cube))
[1] "n"    "pow"
> get("n", environment(cube))
[1] 3
```

We can also take a look at the square() function.

```
> ls(environment(square))
[1] "n"    "pow"
> get("n", environment(square))
[1] 2
```

16.4 Lexical vs. Dynamic Scoping

We can use the following example to demonstrate the difference between lexical and dynamic scoping rules.

```
> y <- 10
>
> f <- function(x) {
+         y <- 2
+         y^2 + g(x)
+ }
>
> g <- function(x) {
+         x*y
+ }
```

What is the value of the following expression?

`f(3)`

With lexical scoping the value of y in the function g is looked up in the environment in which the function was defined, in this case the global environment, so the value of y is 10. With dynamic scoping, the value of y is looked up in the environment from which the function was *called* (sometimes referred to as the *calling environment*). In R the calling environment is known as the *parent frame*. In this case, the value of y would be 2.

When a function is *defined* in the global environment and is subsequently *called* from the global environment, then the defining environment and the calling environment are the same. This can sometimes give the appearance of dynamic scoping.

Consider this example.

```
> g <- function(x) {
+         a <- 3
+         x+a+y
+         ## 'y' is a free variable
+ }
> g(2)
Error in g(2): object 'y' not found
> y <- 3
> g(2)
[1] 8
```

Here, y is defined in the global environment, which also happens to be where the function g() is defined.

There are numerous other languages that support lexical scoping, including

- Scheme

- Perl
- Python
- Common Lisp (all languages converge to Lisp, right?)

Lexical scoping in R has consequences beyond how free variables are looked up. In particular, it's the reason that all objects must be stored in memory in R. This is because all functions must carry a pointer to their respective defining environments, which could be *anywhere*. In the S language (R's close cousin), free variables are always looked up in the global workspace, so everything can be stored on the disk because the "defining environment" of all functions is the same.

16.5 Application: Optimization

Watch a video of this section[4]

NOTE: This section requires some knowledge of statistical inference and modeling. If you do not have such knowledge, feel free to skip this section.

Why is any of this information about lexical scoping useful?

Optimization routines in R like `optim()`, `nlm()`, and `optimize()` require you to pass a function whose argument is a vector of parameters (e.g. a log-likelihood, or a cost function). However, an objective function that needst to be minimized might depend on a host of other things besides its parameters (like data). When writing software which does optimization, it may also be desirable to allow the user to hold certain parameters fixed. The scoping rules of R allow you to abstract away much of the complexity involved in these kinds of problems.

Here is an example of a "constructor" function that creates a negative log-likelihood function that can be minimized to find maximum likelihood estimates in a statistical model.

```
> make.NegLogLik <- function(data, fixed = c(FALSE, FALSE)) {
+         params <- fixed
+         function(p) {
+                 params[!fixed] <- p
+                 mu <- params[1]
+                 sigma <- params[2]
+
+                 ## Calculate the Normal density
+                 a <- -0.5*length(data)*log(2*pi*sigma^2)
+                 b <- -0.5*sum((data-mu)^2) / (sigma^2)
+                 -(a + b)
+         }
+ }
```

---

[4]https://youtu.be/GCNZrffYLFI

Note: Optimization functions in R *minimize* functions, so you need to use the negative log-likelihood.

Now we can generate some data and then construct our negative log-likelihood.

```
> set.seed(1)
> normals <- rnorm(100, 1, 2)
> nLL <- make.NegLogLik(normals)
> nLL
function(p) {
                params[!fixed] <- p
                mu <- params[1]
                sigma <- params[2]

                ## Calculate the Normal density
                a <- -0.5*length(data)*log(2*pi*sigma^2)
                b <- -0.5*sum((data-mu)^2) / (sigma^2)
                -(a + b)
        }
<environment: 0x7fbe630e8d80>
>
> ## What's in the function environment?
> ls(environment(nLL))
[1] "data"   "fixed"   "params"
```

Now that we have our `nLL()` function, we can try to minimize it with `optim()` to estimate the parameters.

```
> optim(c(mu = 0, sigma = 1), nLL)$par
      mu    sigma
1.218239 1.787343
```

You can see that the algorithm converged and obtained an estimate of `mu` and `sigma`.

We can also try to estimate one parameter while holding another parameter fixed. Here we fix `sigma` to be equal to 2.

```
> nLL <- make.NegLogLik(normals, c(FALSE, 2))
> optimize(nLL, c(-1, 3))$minimum
[1] 1.217775
```

Because we now have a one-dimensional problem, we can use the simpler `optimize()` function rather than `optim()`.

We can also try to estimate `sigma` while holding `mu` fixed at 1.

```
> nLL <- make.NegLogLik(normals, c(1, FALSE))
> optimize(nLL, c(1e-6, 10))$minimum
[1] 1.800596
```

16.6 Plotting the Likelihood

Another nice feature that you can take advantage of is plotting the negative log-likelihood to see how peaked or flat it is.

Here is the function when mu is fixed.

```
> ## Fix 'mu' to be equalt o 1
> nLL <- make.NegLogLik(normals, c(1, FALSE))
> x <- seq(1.7, 1.9, len = 100)
>
> ## Evaluate 'nLL()' at every point in 'x'
> y <- sapply(x, nLL)
> plot(x, exp(-(y - min(y))), type = "l")
```

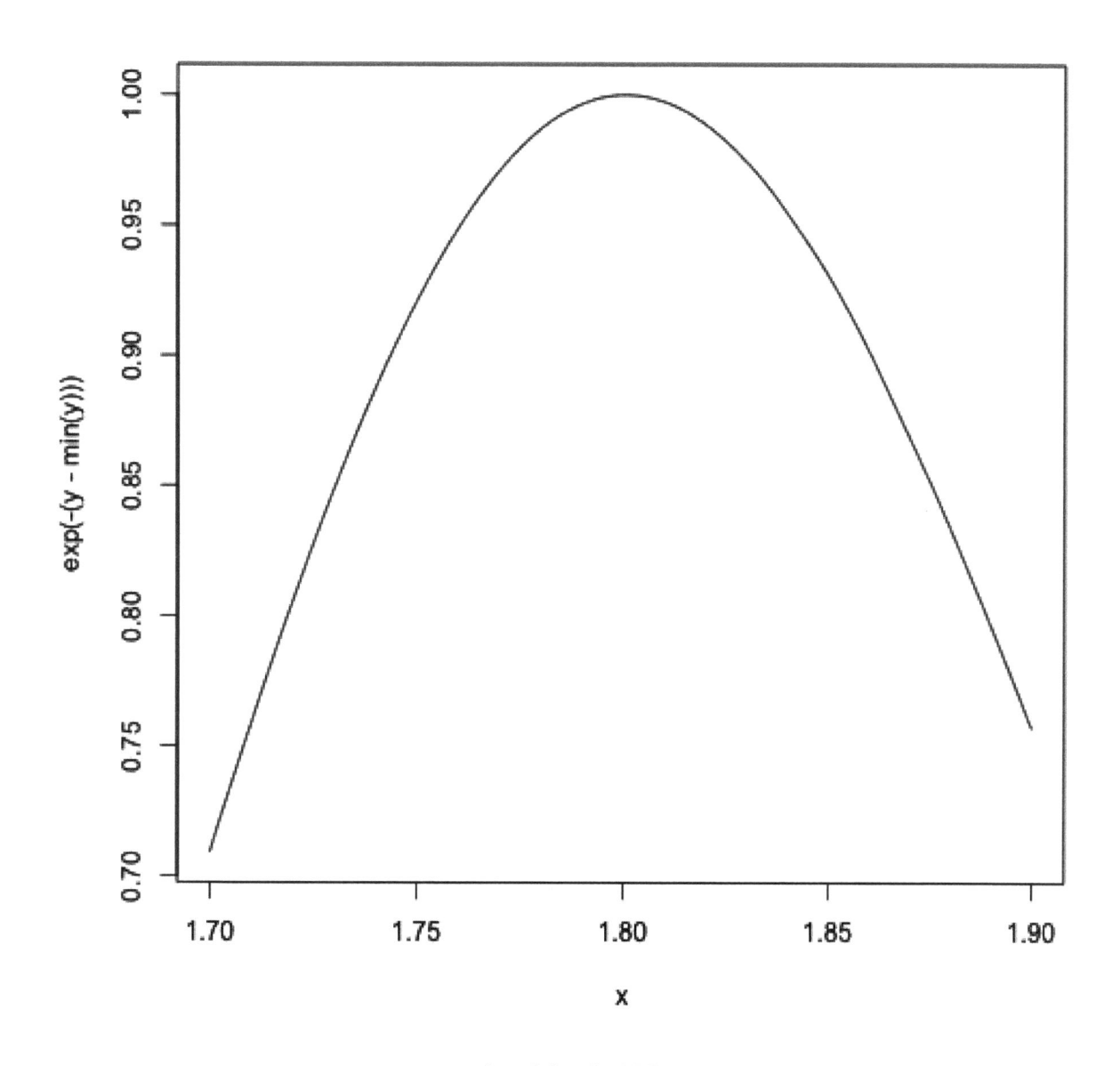

plot of chunk nLLFixMu

Here is the function when sigma is fixed.

```
> ## Fix 'sigma' to be equal to 2
> nLL <- make.NegLogLik(normals, c(FALSE, 2))
> x <- seq(0.5, 1.5, len = 100)
>
> ## Evaluate 'nLL()' at every point in 'x'
> y <- sapply(x, nLL)
> plot(x, exp(-(y - min(y))), type = "l")
```

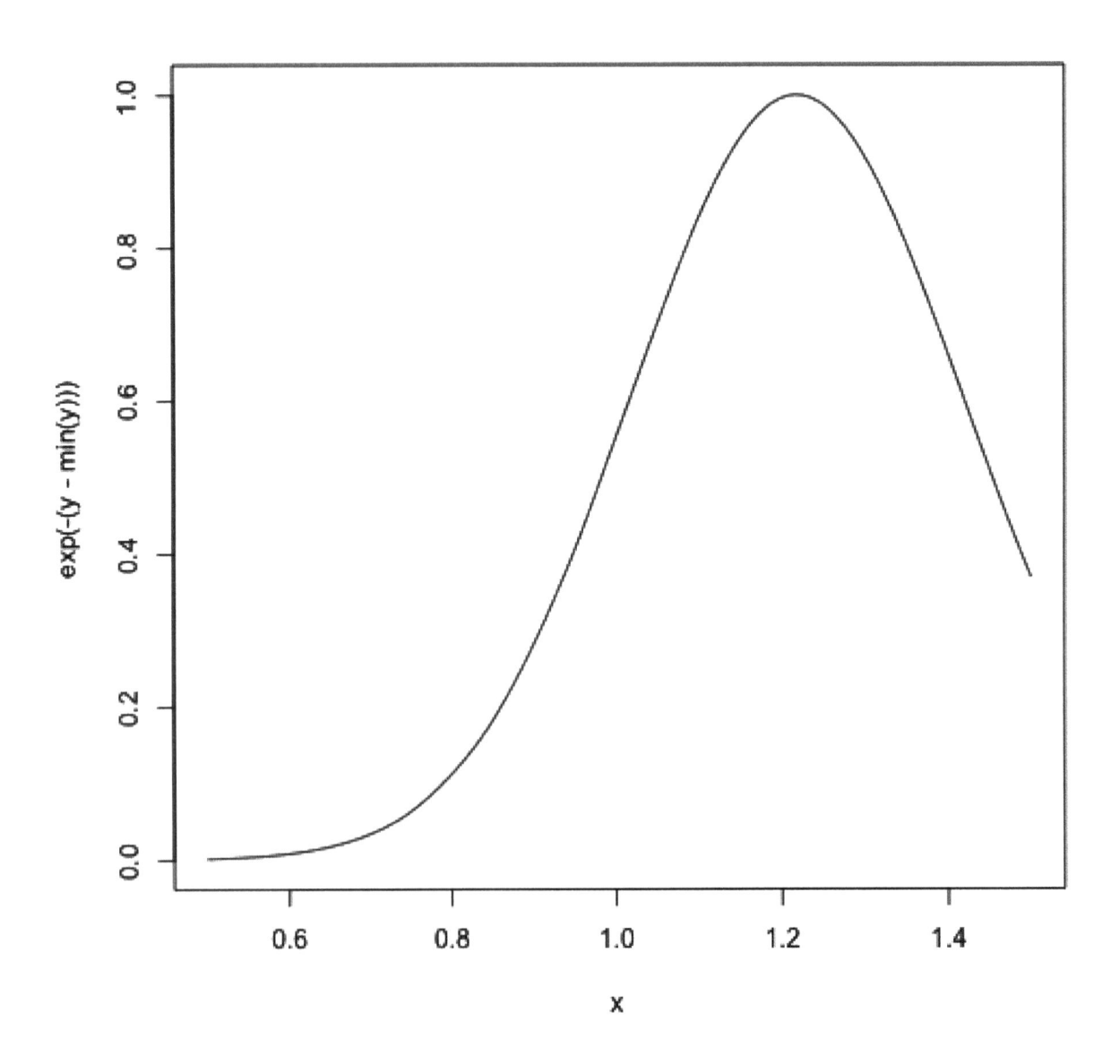

plot of chunk nLLFixSigma

16.7 Summary

- Objective functions can be "built" which contain all of the necessary data for evaluating the function
- No need to carry around long argument lists — useful for interactive and exploratory work.
- Code can be simplified and cleaned up
- Reference: Robert Gentleman and Ross Ihaka (2000). "Lexical Scope and Statistical Computing," *JCGS*, 9, 491–508.

17. Coding Standards for R

Watch a video of this chapter[1]

Coding standards are by no means universal and are often the subject of irrational flame wars on various language- or project-specfiic mailing lists. Nevertheless, I will just give you the standards that I use and the rationale behind them.

Always use text files / text editor. I think we can all agree on this one. Using text files and a text editor is fundamental to coding. If you're writing your code in an editor like Microsoft Word, you need to stop. Interactive development environments like RStudio have nice text editors built in, but there are many others out there.

Indent your code. Indenting is very important for the readability of your code. Some programming languages actually require it as part of their syntax, but R does not. Nevertheless, indenting is very important. How much you should indent is up for debate, but I think each indent should be a minimum of 4 spaces, and ideally **it should be 8 spaces**.

Limit the width of your code. I like to limit the width of my text editor so that the code I write doesn't fly off into the wilderness on the right hand side. This limitation, along with the 8 space indentation, forces you to write code that is clean, readable, and naturally broken down into modular units. In particular, this combination limits your ability to write very long functions with many different levels of nesting.

Limit the length of individual functions. If you are writing functions, it's usually a good idea to not let your functions run for pages and pages. Typically, purpose of a function is to execute one activity or idea. If your function is doing lots of things, it probably needs to be broken into multiple functions. My rule of thumb is that a function should not take up more than one page of your editor (of course, this depends on the size of your monitor).

---

[1]http://youtu.be/MSPKE1y3cyQ

18. Loop Functions

18.1 Looping on the Command Line

Writing for and while loops is useful when programming but not particularly easy when working interactively on the command line. Multi-line expressions with curly braces are just not that easy to sort through when working on the command line. R has some functions which implement looping in a compact form to make your life easier.

- lapply(): Loop over a list and evaluate a function on each element
- sapply(): Same as lapply but try to simplify the result
- apply(): Apply a function over the margins of an array
- tapply(): Apply a function over subsets of a vector
- mapply(): Multivariate version of lapply

An auxiliary function split is also useful, particularly in conjunction with lapply.

18.2 lapply()

Watch a video of this section[1]

The lapply() function does the following simple series of operations:

1. it loops over a list, iterating over each element in that list
2. it applies a *function* to each element of the list (a function that you specify)
3. and returns a list (the l is for "list").

This function takes three arguments: (1) a list X; (2) a function (or the name of a function) FUN; (3) other arguments via its ... argument. If X is not a list, it will be coerced to a list using as.list().

The body of the lapply() function can be seen here.

---

[1]https://youtu.be/E1_NlFb0E4g

```
> lapply
function (X, FUN, ...)
{
    FUN <- match.fun(FUN)
    if (!is.vector(X) || is.object(X))
        X <- as.list(X)
    .Internal(lapply(X, FUN))
}
<bytecode: 0x7f8831140390>
<environment: namespace:base>
```

Note that the actual looping is done internally in C code for efficiency reasons.

It's important to remember that lapply() always returns a list, regardless of the class of the input.

Here's an example of applying the mean() function to all elements of a list. If the original list has names, the the names will be preserved in the output.

```
> x <- list(a = 1:5, b = rnorm(10))
> lapply(x, mean)
$a
[1] 3

$b
[1] 0.1322028
```

Notice that here we are passing the mean() function as an argument to the lapply() function. Functions in R can be used this way and can be passed back and forth as arguments just like any other object. When you pass a function to another function, you do not need to include the open and closed parentheses () like you do when you are *calling* a function.

Here is another example of using lapply().

```
> x <- list(a = 1:4, b = rnorm(10), c = rnorm(20, 1), d = rnorm(100, 5))
> lapply(x, mean)
$a
[1] 2.5

$b
[1] 0.248845

$c
[1] 0.9935285

$d
[1] 5.051388
```

You can use lapply() to evaluate a function multiple times each with a different argument. Below, is an example where I call the runif() function (to generate uniformly distributed random variables) four times, each time generating a different number of random numbers.

```
> x <- 1:4
> lapply(x, runif)
[[1]]
[1] 0.02778712

[[2]]
[1] 0.5273108 0.8803191

[[3]]
[1] 0.37306337 0.04795913 0.13862825

[[4]]
[1] 0.3214921 0.1548316 0.1322282 0.2213059
```

When you pass a function to lapply(), lapply() takes elements of the list and passes them as the *first argument* of the function you are applying. In the above example, the first argument of runif() is n, and so the elements of the sequence 1:4 all got passed to the n argument of runif().

Functions that you pass to lapply() may have other arguments. For example, the runif() function has a min and max argument too. In the example above I used the default values for min and max. How would you be able to specify different values for that in the context of lapply()?

Here is where the ... argument to lapply() comes into play. Any arguments that you place in the ... argument will get passed down to the function being applied to the elements of the list.

Here, the min = 0 and max = 10 arguments are passed down to runif() every time it gets called.

```
> x <- 1:4
> lapply(x, runif, min = 0, max = 10)
[[1]]
[1] 2.263808

[[2]]
[1] 1.314165 9.815635

[[3]]
[1] 3.270137 5.069395 6.814425

[[4]]
[1] 0.9916910 1.1890256 0.5043966 9.2925392
```

So now, instead of the random numbers being between 0 and 1 (the default), the are all between 0 and 10.

The `lapply()` function and its friends make heavy use of *anonymous* functions. Anonymous functions are like members of Project Mayhem[2]—they have no names. These are functions are generated "on the fly" as you are using `lapply()`. Once the call to `lapply()` is finished, the function disappears and does not appear in the workspace.

Here I am creating a list that contains two matrices.

```
> x <- list(a = matrix(1:4, 2, 2), b = matrix(1:6, 3, 2))
> x
$a
     [,1] [,2]
[1,]    1    3
[2,]    2    4

$b
     [,1] [,2]
[1,]    1    4
[2,]    2    5
[3,]    3    6
```

Suppose I wanted to extract the first column of each matrix in the list. I could write an anonymous function for extracting the first column of each matrix.

```
> lapply(x, function(elt) { elt[,1] })
$a
[1] 1 2

$b
[1] 1 2 3
```

Notice that I put the `function()` definition right in the call to `lapply()`. This is perfectly legal and acceptable. You can put an arbitrarily complicated function definition inside `lapply()`, but if it's going to be more complicated, it's probably a better idea to define the function separately.

For example, I could have done the following.

---

[2]http://en.wikipedia.org/wiki/Fight_Club

```
> f <- function(elt) {
+         elt[, 1]
+ }
> lapply(x, f)
$a
[1] 1 2

$b
[1] 1 2 3
```

Now the function is no longer anonymous; it's name is f. Whether you use an anonymous function or you define a function first depends on your context. If you think the function f is something you're going to need a lot in other parts of your code, you might want to define it separately. But if you're just going to use it for this call to lapply(), then it's probably simpler to use an anonymous function.

18.3 sapply()

The sapply() function behaves similarly to lapply(); the only real difference is in the return value. sapply() will try to simplify the result of lapply() if possible. Essentially, sapply() calls lapply() on its input and then applies the following algorithm:

- If the result is a list where every element is length 1, then a vector is returned
- If the result is a list where every element is a vector of the same length (> 1), a matrix is returned.
- If it can't figure things out, a list is returned

Here's the result of calling lapply().

```
> x <- list(a = 1:4, b = rnorm(10), c = rnorm(20, 1), d = rnorm(100, 5))
> lapply(x, mean)
$a
[1] 2.5

$b
[1] -0.251483

$c
[1] 1.481246

$d
[1] 4.968715
```

Notice that lapply() returns a list (as usual), but that each element of the list has length 1.

Here's the result of calling sapply() on the same list.

```
> sapply(x, mean)
       a         b         c         d
2.500000 -0.251483  1.481246  4.968715
```

Because the result of lapply() was a list where each element had length 1, sapply() collapsed the output into a numeric vector, which is often more useful than a list.

18.4 split()

Watch a video of this section[3]

The split() function takes a vector or other objects and splits it into groups determined by a factor or list of factors.

The arguments to split() are

```
> str(split)
function (x, f, drop = FALSE, ...)
```

where

- x is a vector (or list) or data frame
- f is a factor (or coerced to one) or a list of factors
- drop indicates whether empty factors levels should be dropped

The combination of split() and a function like lapply() or sapply() is a common paradigm in R. The basic idea is that you can take a data structure, split it into subsets defined by another variable, and apply a function over those subsets. The results of applying tha function over the subsets are then collated and returned as an object. This sequence of operations is sometimes referred to as "map-reduce" in other contexts.

Here we simulate some data and split it according to a factor variable. Note that we use the gl() function to "generate levels" in a factor variable.

---

[3]https://youtu.be/TjwE5b0fOcs

```
> x <- c(rnorm(10), runif(10), rnorm(10, 1))
> f <- gl(3, 10)
> split(x, f)
$`1`
 [1]  0.3981302 -0.4075286  1.3242586 -0.7012317 -0.5806143 -1.0010722
 [7] -0.6681786  0.9451850  0.4337021  1.0051592

$`2`
 [1] 0.34822440 0.94893818 0.64667919 0.03527777 0.59644846 0.41531800
 [7] 0.07689704 0.52804888 0.96233331 0.70874005

$`3`
 [1]  1.13444766  1.76559900  1.95513668  0.94943430  0.69418458
 [6]  1.89367370 -0.04729815  2.97133739  0.61636789  2.65414530
```

A common idiom is split followed by an lapply.

```
> lapply(split(x, f), mean)
$`1`
[1] 0.07478098

$`2`
[1] 0.5266905

$`3`
[1] 1.458703
```

18.5 Splitting a Data Frame

```
> library(datasets)
> head(airquality)
  Ozone Solar.R Wind Temp Month Day
1    41     190  7.4   67     5   1
2    36     118  8.0   72     5   2
3    12     149 12.6   74     5   3
4    18     313 11.5   62     5   4
5    NA      NA 14.3   56     5   5
6    28      NA 14.9   66     5   6
```

We can split the airquality data frame by the Month variable so that we have separate sub-data frames for each month.

```
> s <- split(airquality, airquality$Month)
> str(s)
List of 5
 $ 5:'data.frame':       31 obs. of  6 variables:
  ..$ Ozone  : int [1:31] 41 36 12 18 NA 28 23 19 8 NA ...
  ..$ Solar.R: int [1:31] 190 118 149 313 NA NA 299 99 19 194 ...
  ..$ Wind   : num [1:31] 7.4 8 12.6 11.5 14.3 14.9 8.6 13.8 20.1 8.6 ...
  ..$ Temp   : int [1:31] 67 72 74 62 56 66 65 59 61 69 ...
  ..$ Month  : int [1:31] 5 5 5 5 5 5 5 5 5 5 ...
  ..$ Day    : int [1:31] 1 2 3 4 5 6 7 8 9 10 ...
 $ 6:'data.frame':       30 obs. of  6 variables:
  ..$ Ozone  : int [1:30] NA NA NA NA NA NA 29 NA 71 39 ...
  ..$ Solar.R: int [1:30] 286 287 242 186 220 264 127 273 291 323 ...
  ..$ Wind   : num [1:30] 8.6 9.7 16.1 9.2 8.6 14.3 9.7 6.9 13.8 11.5 ...
  ..$ Temp   : int [1:30] 78 74 67 84 85 79 82 87 90 87 ...
  ..$ Month  : int [1:30] 6 6 6 6 6 6 6 6 6 6 ...
  ..$ Day    : int [1:30] 1 2 3 4 5 6 7 8 9 10 ...
 $ 7:'data.frame':       31 obs. of  6 variables:
  ..$ Ozone  : int [1:31] 135 49 32 NA 64 40 77 97 97 85 ...
  ..$ Solar.R: int [1:31] 269 248 236 101 175 314 276 267 272 175 ...
  ..$ Wind   : num [1:31] 4.1 9.2 9.2 10.9 4.6 10.9 5.1 6.3 5.7 7.4 ...
  ..$ Temp   : int [1:31] 84 85 81 84 83 83 88 92 92 89 ...
  ..$ Month  : int [1:31] 7 7 7 7 7 7 7 7 7 7 ...
  ..$ Day    : int [1:31] 1 2 3 4 5 6 7 8 9 10 ...
 $ 8:'data.frame':       31 obs. of  6 variables:
  ..$ Ozone  : int [1:31] 39 9 16 78 35 66 122 89 110 NA ...
  ..$ Solar.R: int [1:31] 83 24 77 NA NA NA 255 229 207 222 ...
  ..$ Wind   : num [1:31] 6.9 13.8 7.4 6.9 7.4 4.6 4 10.3 8 8.6 ...
  ..$ Temp   : int [1:31] 81 81 82 86 85 87 89 90 90 92 ...
  ..$ Month  : int [1:31] 8 8 8 8 8 8 8 8 8 8 ...
  ..$ Day    : int [1:31] 1 2 3 4 5 6 7 8 9 10 ...
 $ 9:'data.frame':       30 obs. of  6 variables:
  ..$ Ozone  : int [1:30] 96 78 73 91 47 32 20 23 21 24 ...
  ..$ Solar.R: int [1:30] 167 197 183 189 95 92 252 220 230 259 ...
  ..$ Wind   : num [1:30] 6.9 5.1 2.8 4.6 7.4 15.5 10.9 10.3 10.9 9.7 ...
  ..$ Temp   : int [1:30] 91 92 93 93 87 84 80 78 75 73 ...
  ..$ Month  : int [1:30] 9 9 9 9 9 9 9 9 9 9 ...
  ..$ Day    : int [1:30] 1 2 3 4 5 6 7 8 9 10 ...
```

Then we can take the column means for `Ozone`, `Solar.R`, and `Wind` for each sub-data frame.

```
> lapply(s, function(x) {
+         colMeans(x[, c("Ozone", "Solar.R", "Wind")])
+ })
$`5`
  Ozone  Solar.R     Wind
     NA       NA 11.62258

$`6`
   Ozone   Solar.R      Wind
      NA 190.16667  10.26667

$`7`
   Ozone    Solar.R       Wind
      NA 216.483871   8.941935

$`8`
  Ozone  Solar.R     Wind
     NA       NA 8.793548

$`9`
  Ozone  Solar.R     Wind
     NA 167.4333  10.1800
```

Using `sapply()` might be better here for a more readable output.

```
> sapply(s, function(x) {
+         colMeans(x[, c("Ozone", "Solar.R", "Wind")])
+ })
                5         6          7        8         9
Ozone          NA        NA         NA       NA        NA
Solar.R        NA 190.16667 216.483871       NA 167.4333
Wind     11.62258  10.26667   8.941935 8.793548  10.1800
```

Unfortunately, there are NAs in the data so we cannot simply take the means of those variables. However, we can tell the `colMeans` function to remove the NAs before computing the mean.

```
> sapply(s, function(x) {
+         colMeans(x[, c("Ozone", "Solar.R", "Wind")],
+                  na.rm = TRUE)
+ })
                 5         6         7         8         9
Ozone     23.61538  29.44444  59.115385  59.961538  31.44828
Solar.R  181.29630 190.16667 216.483871 171.857143 167.43333
Wind      11.62258  10.26667   8.941935   8.793548  10.18000
```

Occasionally, we may want to split an R object according to levels defined in more than one variable. We can do this by creating an interaction of the variables with the interaction() function.

```
> x <- rnorm(10)
> f1 <- gl(2, 5)
> f2 <- gl(5, 2)
> f1
 [1] 1 1 1 1 1 2 2 2 2 2
Levels: 1 2
> f2
 [1] 1 1 2 2 3 3 4 4 5 5
Levels: 1 2 3 4 5
> ## Create interaction of two factors
> interaction(f1, f2)
 [1] 1.1 1.1 1.2 1.2 1.3 2.3 2.4 2.4 2.5 2.5
Levels: 1.1 2.1 1.2 2.2 1.3 2.3 1.4 2.4 1.5 2.5
```

With multiple factors and many levels, creating an interaction can result in many levels that are empty.

```
> str(split(x, list(f1, f2)))
List of 10
 $ 1.1: num [1:2] 1.512 0.083
 $ 2.1: num(0)
 $ 1.2: num [1:2] 0.567 -1.025
 $ 2.2: num(0)
 $ 1.3: num 0.323
 $ 2.3: num 1.04
 $ 1.4: num(0)
 $ 2.4: num [1:2] 0.0991 -0.4541
 $ 1.5: num(0)
 $ 2.5: num [1:2] -0.6558 -0.0359
```

Notice that there are 4 categories with no data. But we can drop empty levels when we call the split() function.

```
> str(split(x, list(f1, f2), drop = TRUE))
List of 6
 $ 1.1: num [1:2] 1.512 0.083
 $ 1.2: num [1:2] 0.567 -1.025
 $ 1.3: num 0.323
 $ 2.3: num 1.04
 $ 2.4: num [1:2] 0.0991 -0.4541
 $ 2.5: num [1:2] -0.6558 -0.0359
```

18.6 tapply

Watch a video of this section[4]

tapply() is used to apply a function over subsets of a vector. It can be thought of as a combination of split() and sapply() for vectors only. I've been told that the "t" in tapply() refers to "table", but that is unconfirmed.

```
> str(tapply)
function (X, INDEX, FUN = NULL, ..., simplify = TRUE)
```

The arguments to tapply() are as follows:

- X is a vector
- INDEX is a factor or a list of factors (or else they are coerced to factors)
- FUN is a function to be applied
- ... contains other arguments to be passed FUN
- simplify, should we simplify the result?

Given a vector of numbers, one simple operation is to take group means.

```
> ## Simulate some data
> x <- c(rnorm(10), runif(10), rnorm(10, 1))
> ## Define some groups with a factor variable
> f <- gl(3, 10)
> f
 [1] 1 1 1 1 1 1 1 1 1 1 2 2 2 2 2 2 2 2 2 2 3 3 3 3 3 3 3 3 3 3
Levels: 1 2 3
> tapply(x, f, mean)
        1         2         3
0.1896235 0.5336667 0.9568236
```

We can also take the group means without simplifying the result, which will give us a list. For functions that return a single value, usually, this is not what we want, but it can be done.

---
[4]https://youtu.be/6YEPWjbk3GA

```
> tapply(x, f, mean, simplify = FALSE)
$`1`
[1] 0.1896235

$`2`
[1] 0.5336667

$`3`
[1] 0.9568236
```

We can also apply functions that return more than a single value. In this case, `tapply()` will not simplify the result and will return a list. Here's an example of finding the range of each sub-group.

```
> tapply(x, f, range)
$`1`
[1] -1.869789  1.497041

$`2`
[1] 0.09515213 0.86723879

$`3`
[1] -0.5690822  2.3644349
```

18.7 `apply()`

Watch a video of this section[5]

The `apply()` function is used to a evaluate a function (often an anonymous one) over the margins of an array. It is most often used to apply a function to the rows or columns of a matrix (which is just a 2-dimensional array). However, it can be used with general arrays, for example, to take the average of an array of matrices. Using `apply()` is not really faster than writing a loop, but it works in one line and is highly compact.

```
> str(apply)
function (X, MARGIN, FUN, ...)
```

The arguments to `apply()` are

- X is an array
- `MARGIN` is an integer vector indicating which margins should be "retained".
- `FUN` is a function to be applied
- ... is for other arguments to be passed to `FUN`

Here I create a 20 by 10 matrix of Normal random numbers. I then compute the mean of each column.

---
[5] https://youtu.be/F54ixFPq_xQ

```
> x <- matrix(rnorm(200), 20, 10)
> apply(x, 2, mean)    ## Take the mean of each column
[1]  0.02218266 -0.15932850  0.09021391  0.14723035 -0.22431309
[6] -0.49657847  0.30095015  0.07703985 -0.20818099  0.06809774
```

I can also compute the sum of each row.

```
> apply(x, 1, sum)    ## Take the mean of each row
 [1] -0.48483448  5.33222301 -3.33862932 -1.39998450  2.37859098
 [6]  0.01082604 -6.29457190 -0.26287700  0.71133578 -3.38125293
[11] -4.67522818  3.01900232 -2.39466347 -2.16004389  5.33063755
[16] -2.92024635  3.52026401 -1.84880901 -4.10213912  5.30667310
```

Note that in both calls to `apply()`, the return value was a vector of numbers.

You've probably noticed that the second argument is either a 1 or a 2, depending on whether we want row statistics or column statistics. What exactly *is* the second argument to `apply()`?

The `MARGIN` argument essentially indicates to `apply()` which dimension of the array you want to preserve or retain. So when taking the mean of each column, I specify

```
> apply(x, 2, mean)
```

because I want to collapse the first dimension (the rows) by taking the mean and I want to preserve the number of columns. Similarly, when I want the row sums, I run

```
> apply(x, 1, mean)
```

because I want to collapse the columns (the second dimension) and preserve the number of rows (the first dimension).

18.8 Col/Row Sums and Means

For the special case of column/row sums and column/row means of matrices, we have some useful shortcuts.

- rowSums = `apply(x, 1, sum)`
- rowMeans = `apply(x, 1, mean)`
- colSums = `apply(x, 2, sum)`
- colMeans = `apply(x, 2, mean)`

The shortcut functions are heavily optimized and hence are *much* faster, but you probably won't notice unless you're using a large matrix. Another nice aspect of these functions is that they are a bit more descriptive. It's arguably more clear to write `colMeans(x)` in your code than `apply(x, 2, mean)`.

18.9 Other Ways to Apply

You can do more than take sums and means with the `apply()` function. For example, you can compute quantiles of the rows of a matrix using the `quantile()` function.

```
> x <- matrix(rnorm(200), 20, 10)
> ## Get row quantiles
> apply(x, 1, quantile, probs = c(0.25, 0.75))
          [,1]       [,2]      [,3]       [,4]       [,5]        [,6]
25% -1.0884151 -0.6693040 0.2908481 -0.4602083 -1.0432010 -1.12773555
75%  0.1843547  0.8210295 1.3667301  0.4424153  0.3571219  0.03653687
          [,7]       [,8]       [,9]      [,10]      [,11]       [,12]
25% -1.4571706 -0.2406991 -0.3226845 -0.329898 -0.8677524 -0.2023664
75% -0.1705336  0.6504486  1.1460854  1.247092  0.4138139  0.9145331
         [,13]      [,14]      [,15]       [,16]      [,17]      [,18]
25% -0.9796050 -1.3551031 -0.1823252 -1.260911898 -0.9954289 -0.3767354
75%  0.5448777 -0.5396766  0.7795571  0.002908451  0.4323192  0.7542638
         [,19]      [,20]
25% -0.8557544 -0.7000363
75%  0.5440158  0.5432995
```

Notice that I had to pass the `probs = c(0.25, 0.75)` argument to `quantile()` via the ... argument to `apply()`.

For a higher dimensional example, I can create an array of 2×2 matrices and the compute the average of the matrices in the array.

```
> a <- array(rnorm(2 * 2 * 10), c(2, 2, 10))
> apply(a, c(1, 2), mean)
          [,1]       [,2]
[1,] 0.1681387 -0.1039673
[2,] 0.3519741 -0.4029737
```

In the call to `apply()` here, I indicated via the MARGIN argument that I wanted to preserve the first and second dimensions and to collapse the third dimension by taking the mean.

There is a faster way to do this specific operation via the `colMeans()` function.

```
> rowMeans(a, dims = 2)    ## Faster
          [,1]       [,2]
[1,] 0.1681387 -0.1039673
[2,] 0.3519741 -0.4029737
```

In this situation, I might argue that the use of `rowMeans()` is less readable, but it is substantially faster with large arrays.

18.10 `mapply()`

Watch a video of this section[6]

The `mapply()` function is a multivariate apply of sorts which applies a function in parallel over a set of arguments. Recall that `lapply()` and friends only iterate over a single R object. What if you want to iterate over multiple R objects in parallel? This is what `mapply()` is for.

```
> str(mapply)
function (FUN, ..., MoreArgs = NULL, SIMPLIFY = TRUE, USE.NAMES = TRUE)
```

The arguments to `mapply()` are

- `FUN` is a function to apply
- `...` contains R objects to apply over
- `MoreArgs` is a list of other arguments to `FUN`.
- `SIMPLIFY` indicates whether the result should be simplified

The `mapply()` function has a different argument order from `lapply()` because the function to apply comes first rather than the object to iterate over. The R objects over which we apply the function are given in the ... argument because we can apply over an arbitrary number of R objects.

For example, the following is tedious to type

`list(rep(1, 4), rep(2, 3), rep(3, 2), rep(4, 1))`

With `mapply()`, instead we can do

```
>   mapply(rep, 1:4, 4:1)
[[1]]
[1] 1 1 1 1

[[2]]
[1] 2 2 2

[[3]]
[1] 3 3

[[4]]
[1] 4
```

This passes the sequence `1:4` to the first argument of `rep()` and the sequence `4:1` to the second argument.

Here's another example for simulating randon Normal variables.

---

[6]https://youtu.be/z8jC_h7S0VE

```
> noise <- function(n, mean, sd) {
+         rnorm(n, mean, sd)
+ }
> ## Simulate 5 randon numbers
> noise(5, 1, 2)
[1] -0.5196913  3.2979182 -0.6849525  1.7828267  2.7827545
>
> ## This only simulates 1 set of numbers, not 5
> noise(1:5, 1:5, 2)
[1] -1.670517  2.796247  2.776826  5.351488  3.422804
```

Here we can use mapply() to pass the sequence 1:5 separately to the noise() function so that we can get 5 sets of random numbers, each with a different length and mean.

```
> mapply(noise, 1:5, 1:5, 2)
[[1]]
[1] 0.8260273

[[2]]
[1] 4.764568 2.336980

[[3]]
[1] 4.6463819 2.5582108 0.9412167

[[4]]
[1]  3.978149  1.550018 -1.192223  6.338245

[[5]]
[1] 2.826182 1.347834 6.990564 4.976276 3.800743
```

The above call to mapply() is the same as

```
> list(noise(1, 1, 2), noise(2, 2, 2),
+      noise(3, 3, 2), noise(4, 4, 2),
+      noise(5, 5, 2))
[[1]]
[1] 0.644104

[[2]]
[1] 1.148037 3.993318

[[3]]
[1]  4.4553214 -0.4532612  3.7067970
```

```
[[4]]
[1]  5.4536273  5.3365220 -0.8486346  3.5292851

[[5]]
[1] 8.959267 6.593589 1.581448 1.672663 5.982219
```

18.11 Vectorizing a Function

The `mapply()` function can be use to automatically "vectorize" a function. What this means is that it can be used to take a function that typically only takes single arguments and create a new function that can take vector arguments. This is often needed when you want to plot functions.

Here's an example of a function that computes the sum of squares given some data, a mean parameter and a standard deviation. The formula is $\sum_{i=1}^{n}(x_i - \mu)^2/\sigma^2$.

```
> sumsq <- function(mu, sigma, x) {
+         sum(((x - mu) / sigma)^2)
+ }
```

This function takes a mean `mu`, a standard deviation `sigma`, and some data in a vector `x`.

In many statistical applications, we want to minimize the sum of squares to find the optimal `mu` and `sigma`. Before we do that, we may want to evaluate or plot the function for many different values of `mu` or `sigma`. However, passing a vector of `mu`s or `sigma`s won't work with this function because it's not vectorized.

```
> x <- rnorm(100)          ## Generate some data
> sumsq(1:10, 1:10, x)     ## This is not what we want
[1] 110.2594
```

Note that the call to `sumsq()` only produced one value instead of 10 values.

However, we can do what we want to do by using `mapply()`.

```
> mapply(sumsq, 1:10, 1:10, MoreArgs = list(x = x))
 [1] 196.2289 121.4765 108.3981 104.0788 102.1975 101.2393 100.6998
 [8] 100.3745 100.1685 100.0332
```

There's even a function in R called `Vectorize()` that automatically can create a vectorized version of your function. So we could create a `vsumsq()` function that is fully vectorized as follows.

```
> vsumsq <- Vectorize(sumsq, c("mu", "sigma"))
> vsumsq(1:10, 1:10, x)
 [1] 196.2289 121.4765 108.3981 104.0788 102.1975 101.2393 100.6998
 [8] 100.3745 100.1685 100.0332
```

Pretty cool, right?

18.12 Summary

- The loop functions in R are very powerful because they allow you to conduct a series of operations on data using a compact form
- The operation of a loop function involves iterating over an R object (e.g. a list or vector or matrix), applying a function to each element of the object, and the collating the results and returning the collated results.
- Loop functions make heavy use of anonymous functions, which exist for the life of the loop function but are not stored anywhere
- The `split()` function can be used to divide an R object in to subsets determined by another variable which can subsequently be looped over using loop functions.

19. Regular Expressions

Watch a video of this chapter[1]

19.1 Before You Begin

If you want a very quick introduction to the general notion of regular expressions and how they can be used to process text (as opposed to how to implement them specifically in R), you should watch this lecture[2] first.

19.2 Primary R Functions

The primary R functions for dealing with regular expressions are

- `grep()`, `grepl()`: These functions search for matches of a regular expression/pattern in a character vector. `grep()` returns the indices into the character vector that contain a match or the specific strings that happen to have the match. `grepl()` returns a TRUE/FALSE vector indicating which elements of the character vector contain a match
- `regexpr()`, `gregexpr()`: Search a character vector for regular expression matches and return the indices of the string where the match begins and the length of the match
- `sub()`, `gsub()`: Search a character vector for regular expression matches and replace that match with another string
- `regexec()`: This function searches a character vector for a regular expression, much like `regexpr()`, but it will additionally return the locations of any parenthesized sub-expressions. Probably easier to explain through demonstration.

For this chapter, we will use a running example using data from homicides in Baltimore City. The Baltimore Sun newspaper collects information on all homicides that occur in the city (it also reports on many of them). That data is collected and presented in a map that is publically available[3]. I encourage you to go look at the web site/map to get a sense of what kinds of data are presented there. Unfortunately, the data on the web site are not particularly amenable to analysis, so I've scraped the data and put it in a separate file. The data in this file contain data from January 2007 to October 2013.

Here is an excerpt of the Baltimore City homicides dataset:

---

[1]https://www.youtube.com/watch?v=q8SzNKib5-4
[2]https://www.youtube.com/watch?v=NvHjYOilOf8
[3]http://data.baltimoresun.com/bing-maps/homicides/

```
> homicides <- readLines("homicides.txt")
>
> ## Total number of events recorded
> length(homicides)
[1] 1571
> homicides[1]
[1] "39.311024, -76.674227, iconHomicideShooting, 'p2', '<dl><dt>Leon Nelson</dt><dd class\
=\"address\">3400 Clifton Ave.<br />Baltimore, MD 21216</dd><dd>black male, 17 years old</\
dd><dd>Found on January 1, 2007</dd><dd>Victim died at Shock Trauma</dd><dd>Cause: shootin\
g</dd></dl>'"
> homicides[1000]
[1] "39.33626300000, -76.55553990000, icon_homicide_shooting, 'p1200', '<dl><dt><a href=\"\
http://essentials.baltimoresun.com/micro_sun/homicides/victim/1200/davon-diggs\">Davon Dig\
gs</a></dt><dd class=\"address\">4100 Parkwood Ave<br />Baltimore, MD 21206</dd><dd>Race: \
Black<br />Gender: male<br />Age: 21 years old</dd><dd>Found on November  5, 2011</dd><dd>\
Victim died at Johns Hopkins Bayview Medical Center </dd><dd>Cause: Shooting</dd><dd class\
=\"popup-note\"><p>Originally reported in 5000 Belair Road; later determined to be rear al\
ley of 4100 block Parkwood</p></dd></dl>'"
```

The data set is formatted so that each homicide is presented on a single line of text. So when we read the data in with readLines(), each element of the character vector represents one homicide event. Notice that the data are riddled with HTML tags because they were scraped directly from the web site.

A few interesting features stand out: We have the latitude and longitude of where the victim was found; then there's the street address; the age, race, and gender of the victim; the date on which the victim was found; in which hospital the victim ultimately died; the cause of death.

19.3 grep()

Suppose we wanted to identify the records for all the victims of shootings (as opposed to other causes)? How could we do that? From the map we know that for each cause of death there is a different icon/flag placed on the map. In particular, they are different colors. You can see that is indicated in the dataset for shooting deaths with a iconHomicideShooting label. Perhaps we can use this aspect of the data to idenfity all of the shootings.

Here I use grep() to match the literal iconHomicideShooting into the character vector of homicides.

```
> g <- grep("iconHomicideShooting", homicides)
> length(g)
[1] 228
```

Using this approach I get 228 shooting deaths. However, I notice that for some of the entries, the indicator for the homicide "flag" is noted as icon_homicide_shooting. It's not uncommon over time for web site maintainers to change the names of files or update files. What happens if we now grep() on both icon names using the | operator?

```
> g <- grep("iconHomicideShooting|icon_homicide_shooting", homicides)
> length(g)
[1] 1263
```

Now we have 1263 shooting deaths, which is quite a bit more. In fact, the vast majority of homicides in Baltimore are shooting deaths.

Another possible way to do this is to grep() on the cause of death field, which seems to have the format Cause: shooting. We can grep() on this literally and get

```
> g <- grep("Cause: shooting", homicides)
> length(g)
[1] 228
```

Notice that we seem to be undercounting again. This is because for some of the entries, the word "shooting" uses a captial "S" while other entries use a lower case "s". We can handle this variation by using a character class in our regular expression.

```
> g <- grep("Cause: [Ss]hooting", homicides)
> length(g)
[1] 1263
```

One thing you have to be careful of when processing text data is not not grep() things out of context. For example, suppose we just grep()-ed on the expression [Ss]hooting.

```
> g <- grep("[Ss]hooting", homicides)
> length(g)
[1] 1265
```

Notice that we see to pick up 2 extra homicides this way. We can figure out which ones they are by comparing the results of the two expressions.

First we can get the indices for the first expresssion match.

```
> i <- grep("[cC]ause: [Ss]hooting", homicides)
> str(i)
 int [1:1263] 1 2 6 7 8 9 10 11 12 13 ...
```

Then we can get the indices for just matching on [Ss]hooting.

```
> j <- grep("[Ss]hooting", homicides)
> str(j)
 int [1:1265] 1 2 6 7 8 9 10 11 12 13 ...
```

Now we just need to identify which are the entries that the vectors i and j do *not* have in common.

```
> setdiff(i, j)
integer(0)
> setdiff(j, i)
[1] 318 859
```

Here we can see that the index vector j has two entries that are not in i: entries 318, 859. We can take a look at these entries directly to see what makes them different.

```
> homicides[859]
[1] "39.33743900000, -76.66316500000, icon_homicide_bluntforce, 'p914', '<dl><dt><a href=\\
"http://essentials.baltimoresun.com/micro_sun/homicides/victim/914/steven-harris\">Steven \
Harris</a></dt><dd class=\"address\">4200 Pimlico Road<br />Baltimore, MD 21215</dd><dd>Ra\
ce: Black<br />Gender: male<br />Age: 38 years old</dd><dd>Found on July 29, 2010</dd><dd>\
Victim died at Scene</dd><dd>Cause: Blunt Force</dd><dd class=\"popup-note\"><p>Harris was\
 found dead July 22 and ruled a shooting victim; an autopsy subsequently showed that he ha\
d not been shot,...</dd></dl>'"
```

Here we can see that the word "shooting" appears in the narrative text that accompanies the data, but the ultimate cause of death was in fact blunt force.

> When developing a regular expression to extract entries from a large dataset, it's important that you understand the formatting of the dataset well enough so that you can develop a specific expression that doesn't accidentally grep data out of context.

Sometimes we want to identify elements of a character vector that match a pattern, but instead of returning their indices we want the actual values that satisfy the match. For example, we may want to identify all of the states in the United States whose names start with "New".

```
> grep("^New", state.name)
[1] 29 30 31 32
```

This gives us the indices into the state.name variable that match, but setting value = TRUE returns the actual elements of the character vector that match.

```
> grep("^New", state.name, value = TRUE)
[1] "New Hampshire" "New Jersey"    "New Mexico"    "New York"
```

19.4 `grepl()`

The function `grepl()` works much like `grep()` except that it differs in its return value. `grepl()` returns a logical vector indicating which element of a character vector contains the match. For example, suppose we want to know which states in the United States begin with word "New".

```
> g <- grepl("^New", state.name)
> g
 [1] FALSE FALSE FALSE FALSE FALSE FALSE FALSE FALSE FALSE FALSE FALSE
[12] FALSE FALSE FALSE FALSE FALSE FALSE FALSE FALSE FALSE FALSE FALSE
[23] FALSE FALSE FALSE FALSE FALSE FALSE  TRUE  TRUE  TRUE  TRUE FALSE
[34] FALSE FALSE FALSE FALSE FALSE FALSE FALSE FALSE FALSE FALSE FALSE
[45] FALSE FALSE FALSE FALSE FALSE FALSE
> state.name[g]
[1] "New Hampshire" "New Jersey"    "New Mexico"    "New York"
```

Here, we can see that `grepl()` returns a logical vector that can be used to subset the original `state.name` vector.

19.5 `regexpr()`

Both the `grep()` and the `grepl()` functions have some limitations. In particular, both functions tell you which strings in a character vector match a certain pattern but they don't tell you exactly where the match occurs or what the match is for a more complicated regular expression.

The `regexpr()` function gives you the (a) index into each string where the match begins and the (b) length of the match for that string. `regexpr()` only gives you the *first* match of the string (reading left to right). `gregexpr()` will give you *all* of the matches in a given string if there are is more than one match.

In our Baltimore City homicides dataset, we might be interested in finding the date on which each victim was found. Taking a look at the dataset

```
> homicides[1]
[1] "39.311024, -76.674227, iconHomicideShooting, 'p2', '<dl><dt>Leon Nelson</dt><dd class\
=\"address\">3400 Clifton Ave.<br />Baltimore, MD 21216</dd><dd>black male, 17 years old</\
dd><dd>Found on January 1, 2007</dd><dd>Victim died at Shock Trauma</dd><dd>Cause: shootin\
g</dd></dl>'"
```

it seems that we might be able to just grep on the word "Found". However, the word "found" may be found elsewhere in the entry, such as in this entry, where the word "found" appears in the narrative text at the end.

```
> homicides[954]
[1] "39.30677400000, -76.59891100000, icon_homicide_shooting, 'p816', '<dl><dt><a href=\"h\
ttp://essentials.baltimoresun.com/micro_sun/homicides/victim/816/kenly-wheeler\">Kenly Whe\
eler</a></dt><dd class=\"address\">1400 N Caroline St<br />Baltimore, MD 21213</dd><dd>Rac\
e: Black<br />Gender: male<br />Age: 29 years old</dd><dd>Found on March  3, 2010</dd><dd>\
Victim died at Scene</dd><dd>Cause: Shooting</dd><dd class=\"popup-note\"><p>Wheeler\\'s b\
ody was found on the grounds of Dr. Bernard Harris Sr. Elementary School</p></dd\
></dl>'"
```

But we can see that the date is typically preceded by "Found on" and is surrounded by <dd></dd> tags, so let's use the pattern <dd>[F|f]ound(.*)</dd> and see what it brings up.

```
> regexpr("<dd>[F|f]ound(.*)</dd>", homicides[1:10])
 [1] 177 178 188 189 178 182 178 187 182 183
attr(,"match.length")
 [1] 93 86 89 90 89 84 85 84 88 84
attr(,"useBytes")
[1] TRUE
```

We can use the substr() function to extract the first match in the first string.

```
> substr(homicides[1], 177, 177 + 93 - 1)
[1] "<dd>Found on January 1, 2007</dd><dd>Victim died at Shock Trauma</dd><dd>Cause: shoot\
ing</dd>"
```

Immediately, we can see that the regular expression picked up too much information. This is because the previous pattern was too greedy and matched too much of the string. We need to use the ? metacharacter to make the regular expression "lazy" so that it stops at the *first* </dd> tag.

```
> regexpr("<dd>[F|f]ound(.*?)</dd>", homicides[1:10])
 [1] 177 178 188 189 178 182 178 187 182 183
attr(,"match.length")
 [1] 33 33 33 33 33 33 33 33 33 33
attr(,"useBytes")
[1] TRUE
```

Now when we look at the substrings indicated by the regexpr() output, we get

```
> substr(homicides[1], 177, 177 + 33 - 1)
[1] "<dd>Found on January 1, 2007</dd>"
```

While it's straightforward to take the output of regexpr() and feed it into substr() to get the matches out of the original data, one handy function is regmatches() which extracts the matches in the strings for you without you having to use substr().

```
> r <- regexpr("<dd>[F|f]ound(.*?)</dd>", homicides[1:5])
> regmatches(homicides[1:5], r)
[1] "<dd>Found on January 1, 2007</dd>" "<dd>Found on January 2, 2007</dd>"
[3] "<dd>Found on January 2, 2007</dd>" "<dd>Found on January 3, 2007</dd>"
[5] "<dd>Found on January 5, 2007</dd>"
```

19.6 sub() and gsub()

Sometimes we need to clean things up or modify strings by matching a pattern and replacing it with something else. For example, how can we extract the date from this string?

```
> x <- substr(homicides[1], 177, 177 + 33 - 1)
> x
[1] "<dd>Found on January 1, 2007</dd>"
```

We want to strip out the stuff surrounding the "January 1, 2007" portion. We can do that by matching on the text that comes before and after it using the | operator and then replacing it with the empty string.

```
> sub("<dd>[F|f]ound on |</dd>", "", x)
[1] "January 1, 2007</dd>"
```

Notice that the sub() function found the first match (at the beginning of the string) and replaced it and then stopped. However, there was another match at the end of the string that we also wanted to replace. To get both matches, we need the gsub() function.

```
> gsub("<dd>[F|f]ound on |</dd>", "", x)
[1] "January 1, 2007"
```

The sub() and gsub()' functions can take vector arguments so we don't have to process each string one by one.

```
> r <- regexpr("<dd>[F|f]ound(.*?)</dd>", homicides[1:5])
> m <- regmatches(homicides[1:5], r)
> m
[1] "<dd>Found on January 1, 2007</dd>" "<dd>Found on January 2, 2007</dd>"
[3] "<dd>Found on January 2, 2007</dd>" "<dd>Found on January 3, 2007</dd>"
[5] "<dd>Found on January 5, 2007</dd>"
> d <- gsub("<dd>[F|f]ound on |</dd>", "", m)
>
> ## Nice and clean
> d
[1] "January 1, 2007" "January 2, 2007" "January 2, 2007" "January 3, 2007"
[5] "January 5, 2007"
```

Finally, it may be useful to convert these strings to the Date class so that we can do some date-related computations.

```
> as.Date(d, "%B %d, %Y")
[1] "2007-01-01" "2007-01-02" "2007-01-02" "2007-01-03" "2007-01-05"
```

19.7 regexec()

The regexec() function works like regexpr() except it gives you the indices for parenthesized subexpressions. For example, take a look at the following expression.

```
> regexec("<dd>[F|f]ound on (.*?)</dd>", homicides[1])
[[1]]
[1] 177 190
attr(,"match.length")
[1] 33 15
```

Notice first that the regular expression itself has a portion in parentheses (). That is the portion of the expression that I presume will contain the date. In the output, you'll notice that there are two indices and two "match.length" values. The first index tells you where the overall match begins (character 177) and the second index tells you where the expression in the parentheses begins (character 190).

By contrast, if we only use the regexpr() function, we get

```
> regexec("<dd>[F|f]ound on .*?</dd>", homicides[1])
[[1]]
[1] 177
attr(,"match.length")
[1] 33
```

We can use the `substr()` function to demonstrate which parts of a strings are matched by the `regexec()` function.

Here's the output for `regexec()`.

```
> regexec("<dd>[F|f]ound on (.*?)</dd>", homicides[1])
[[1]]
[1] 177 190
attr(,"match.length")
[1] 33 15
```

Here's the overall expression match.

```
> substr(homicides[1], 177, 177 + 33 - 1)
[1] "<dd>Found on January 1, 2007</dd>"
```

And here's the parenthesized sub-expression.

```
> substr(homicides[1], 190, 190 + 15 - 1)
[1] "January 1, 2007"
```

All this can be done much more easily with the `regmatches()` function.

```
> r <- regexec("<dd>[F|f]ound on (.*?)</dd>", homicides[1:2])
> regmatches(homicides[1:2], r)
[[1]]
[1] "<dd>Found on January 1, 2007</dd>" "January 1, 2007"

[[2]]
[1] "<dd>Found on January 2, 2007</dd>" "January 2, 2007"
```

Notice that `regmatches()` returns a list in this case, where each element of the list contains two strings: the overall match and the parenthesized sub-expression.

As an example, we can make a plot of monthly homicide counts. First we need a regular expression to capture the dates.

```
> r <- regexec("<dd>[F|f]ound on (.*?)</dd>", homicides)
> m <- regmatches(homicides, r)
```

Then we can loop through the list returned by regmatches() and extract the second element of each (the parenthesized sub-expression).

```
> dates <- sapply(m, function(x) x[2])
```

Finally, we can convert the date strings into the Date class and make a histogram of the counts.

```
> dates <- as.Date(dates, "%B %d, %Y")
> hist(dates, "month", freq = TRUE, main = "Monthly Homicides in Baltimore")
```

Monthly Homicides in Baltimore

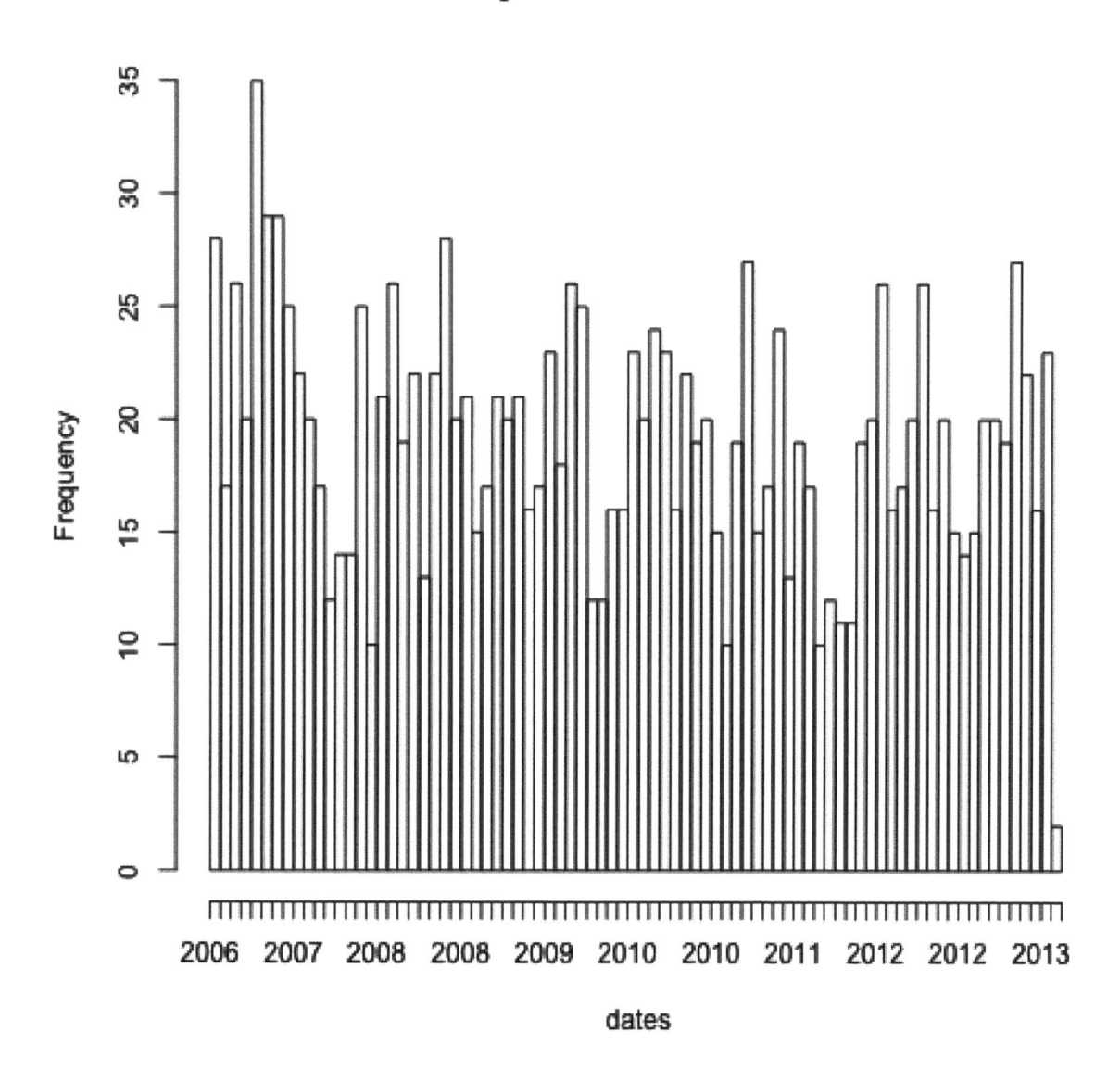

plot of chunk unnamed-chunk-35

We can see from the picture that homicides do not occur uniformly throughout the year and appear to have some seasonality to them.

19.8 Summary

The primary R functions for dealing with regular expressions are

- `grep()`, `grepl()`: Search for matches of a regular expression/pattern in a character vector

- `regexpr()`,`gregexpr()`: Search a character vector for regular expression matches and return the indices where the match begins; useful in conjunction with regmatches()'
- `sub()`,`gsub()`: Search a character vector for regular expression matches and replace that match with another string
- `regexec()`: Gives you indices of parethensized sub-expressions.

20. Debugging

20.1 Something's Wrong!

Watch a video of this section[1] (note that this video differs slightly from the material presented here)

R has a number of ways to indicate to you that something's not right. There are different levels of indication that can be used, ranging from mere notification to fatal error. Executing any function in R may result in the following *conditions*.

- `message`: A generic notification/diagnostic message produced by the `message()` function; execution of the function continues
- `warning`: An indication that something is wrong but not necessarily fatal; execution of the function continues. Warnings are generated by the `warning()` function
- `error`: An indication that a fatal problem has occurred and execution of the function stops. Errors are produced by the `stop()` function.
- `condition`: A generic concept for indicating that something unexpected has occurred; programmers can create their own custom conditions if they want.

Here is an example of a warning that you might receive in the course of using R.

```
> log(-1)
Warning in log(-1): NaNs produced
[1] NaN
```

This warning lets you know that taking the log of a negative number results in a `NaN` value because you can't take the log of negative numbers. Nevertheless, R doesn't give an error, because it has a useful value that it can return, the `NaN` value. The warning is just there to let you know that something unexpected happen. Depending on what you are programming, you may have intentionally taken the log of a negative number in order to move on to another section of code.

Here is another function that is designed to print a message to the console depending on the nature of its input.

---

[1]https://youtu.be/LHQxbRInyyc

```
> printmessage <- function(x) {
+         if(x > 0)
+                 print("x is greater than zero")
+         else
+                 print("x is less than or equal to zero")
+         invisible(x)
+ }
```

This function is simple—it prints a message telling you whether x is greater than zero or less than or equal to zero. It also returns its input *invisibly*, which is a common practice with "print" functions. Returning an object invisibly means that the return value does not get auto-printed when the function is called.

Take a hard look at the function above and see if you can identify any bugs or problems.

We can execute the function as follows.

```
> printmessage(1)
[1] "x is greater than zero"
```

The function seems to work fine at this point. No errors, warnings, or messages.

```
> printmessage(NA)
Error in if (x > 0) print("x is greater than zero") else print("x is less than or equal to\
 zero"): missing value where TRUE/FALSE needed
```

What happened?

Well, the first thing the function does is test if x > 0. But you can't do that test if x is a NA or NaN value. R doesn't know what to do in this case so it stops with a fatal error.

We can fix this problem by anticipating the possibility of NA values and checking to see if the input is NA with the is.na() function.

```
> printmessage2 <- function(x) {
+         if(is.na(x))
+                 print("x is a missing value!")
+         else if(x > 0)
+                 print("x is greater than zero")
+         else
+                 print("x is less than or equal to zero")
+         invisible(x)
+ }
```

Now we can run the following.

```
> printmessage2(NA)
[1] "x is a missing value!"
```

And all is fine.

Now what about the following situation.

```
> x <- log(c(-1, 2))
Warning in log(c(-1, 2)): NaNs produced
> printmessage2(x)
Warning in if (is.na(x)) print("x is a missing value!") else if (x > 0)
print("x is greater than zero") else print("x is less than or equal to
zero"): the condition has length > 1 and only the first element will be
used
[1] "x is a missing value!"
```

Now what?? Why are we getting this warning? The warning says "the condition has length > 1 and only the first element will be used".

The problem here is that I passed `printmessage2()` a vector `x` that was of length 2 rather then length 1. Inside the body of `printmessage2()` the expression `is.na(x)` returns a vector that is tested in the `if` statement. However, `if` cannot take vector arguments so you get a warning. The fundamental problem here is that `printmessage2()` is not *vectorized*.

We can solve this problem two ways. One is by simply not allowing vector arguments. The other way is to vectorize the `printmessage2()` function to allow it to take vector arguments.

For the first way, we simply need to check the length of the input.

```
> printmessage3 <- function(x) {
+         if(length(x) > 1L)
+                 stop("'x' has length > 1")
+         if(is.na(x))
+                 print("x is a missing value!")
+         else if(x > 0)
+                 print("x is greater than zero")
+         else
+                 print("x is less than or equal to zero")
+         invisible(x)
+ }
```

Now when we pass `printmessage3()` a vector we should get an error.

```
> printmessage3(1:2)
Error in printmessage3(1:2): 'x' has length > 1
```

Vectorizing the function can be accomplished easily with the `Vectorize()` function.

```
> printmessage4 <- Vectorize(printmessage2)
> out <- printmessage4(c(-1, 2))
[1] "x is less than or equal to zero"
[1] "x is greater than zero"
```

You can see now that the correct messages are printed without any warning or error. Note that I stored the return value of `printmessage4()` in a separate R object called `out`. This is because when I use the `Vectorize()` function it no longer preserves the invisibility of the return value.

20.2 Figuring Out What's Wrong

The primary task of debugging any R code is correctly diagnosing what the problem is. When diagnosing a problem with your code (or somebody else's), it's important first understand what you were expecting to occur. Then you need to idenfity what *did* occur and how did it deviate from your expectations. Some basic questions you need to ask are

- What was your input? How did you call the function?
- What were you expecting? Output, messages, other results?
- What did you get?
- How does what you get differ from what you were expecting?
- Were your expectations correct in the first place?
- Can you reproduce the problem (exactly)?

Being able to answer these questions is important not just for your own sake, but in situations where you may need to ask someone else for help with debugging the problem. Seasoned programmers will be asking you these exact questions.

20.3 Debugging Tools in R

Watch a video of this section[2]

R provides a number of tools to help you with debugging your code. The primary tools for debugging functions in R are

---

[2]https://youtu.be/h9rs6-Cwwto

- `traceback()`: prints out the function call stack after an error occurs; does nothing if there's no error
- `debug()`: flags a function for "debug" mode which allows you to step through execution of a function one line at a time
- `browser()`: suspends the execution of a function wherever it is called and puts the function in debug mode
- `trace()`: allows you to insert debugging code into a function a specific places
- `recover()`: allows you to modify the error behavior so that you can browse the function call stack

These functions are interactive tools specifically designed to allow you to pick through a function. There's also the more blunt technique of inserting `print()` or `cat()` statements in the function.

20.4 Using `traceback()`

Watch a video of this section[3]

The `traceback()` function prints out the *function call stack* after an error has occurred. The function call stack is the sequence of functions that was called before the error occurred.

For example, you may have a function `a()` which subsequently calls function `b()` which calls `c()` and then `d()`. If an error occurs, it may not be immediately clear in which function the error occurred. The `traceback()` function shows you how many levels deep you were when the error occurred.

```
> mean(x)
Error in mean(x) : object 'x' not found
> traceback()
1: mean(x)
```

Here, it's clear that the error occurred inside the `mean()` function because the object x does not exist.

The `traceback()` function must be called immediately after an error occurs. Once another function is called, you lose the traceback.

Here is a slightly more complicated example using the `lm()` function for linear modeling.

---
[3]https://youtu.be/VT9ZxCp6o-I

```
> lm(y ~ x)
Error in eval(expr, envir, enclos) : object 'y' not found
> traceback()
7: eval(expr, envir, enclos)
6: eval(predvars, data, env)
5: model.frame.default(formula = y ~ x, drop.unused.levels = TRUE)
4: model.frame(formula = y ~ x, drop.unused.levels = TRUE)
3: eval(expr, envir, enclos)
2: eval(mf, parent.frame())
1: lm(y ~ x)
```

You can see now that the error did not get thrown until the 7th level of the function call stack, in which case the `eval()` function tried to evaluate the formula y ~ x and realized the object y did not exist.

Looking at the traceback is useful for figuring out roughly where an error occurred but it's not useful for more detailed debugging. For that you might turn to the `debug()` function.

20.5 Using `debug()`

The `debug()` function initiates an interactive debugger (also known as the "browser" in R) for a function. With the debugger, you can step through an R function one expression at a time to pinpoint exactly where an error occurs.

The `debug()` function takes a function as its first argument. Here is an example of debugging the `lm()` function.

```
> debug(lm)       ## Flag the 'lm()' function for interactive debugging
> lm(y ~ x)
debugging in: lm(y ~ x)
debug: {
    ret.x <- x
    ret.y <- y
    cl <- match.call()
    ...
    if (!qr)
        z$qr <- NULL
    z
}
Browse[2]>
```

Now, every time you call the `lm()` function it will launch the interactive debugger. To turn this behavior off you need to call the `undebug()` function.

The debugger calls the browser at the very top level of the function body. From there you can step through each expression in the body. There are a few special commands you can call in the browser:

- n executes the current expression and moves to the next expression
- c continues execution of the function and does not stop until either an error or the function exits
- Q quits the browser

Here's an example of a browser session with the `lm()` function.

```
Browse[2]> n     ## Evalute this expression and move to the next one
debug: ret.x <- x
Browse[2]> n
debug: ret.y <- y
Browse[2]> n
debug: cl <- match.call()
Browse[2]> n
debug: mf <- match.call(expand.dots = FALSE)
Browse[2]> n
debug: m <- match(c("formula", "data", "subset", "weights", "na.action",
    "offset"), names(mf), 0L)
```

While you are in the browser you can execute any other R function that might be available to you in a regular session. In particular, you can use `ls()` to see what is in your current environment (the function environment) and `print()` to print out the values of R objects in the function environment.

You can turn off interactive debugging with the `undebug()` function.

```
undebug(lm)     ## Unflag the 'lm()' function for debugging
```

20.6 Using `recover()`

The `recover()` function can be used to modify the error behavior of R when an error occurs. Normally, when an error occurs in a function, R will print out an error message, exit out of the function, and return you to your workspace to await further commands.

With `recover()` you can tell R that when an error occurs, it should halt execution at the exact point at which the error occurred. That can give you the opportunity to poke around in the environment in which the error occurred. This can be useful to see if there are any R objects or data that have been corrupted or mistakenly modified.

```
> options(error = recover)     ## Change default R error behavior
> read.csv("nosuchfile")       ## This code doesn't work
Error in file(file, "rt") : cannot open the connection
In addition: Warning message:
In file(file, "rt") :
  cannot open file 'nosuchfile': No such file or directory

Enter a frame number, or 0 to exit

1: read.csv("nosuchfile")
2: read.table(file = file, header = header, sep = sep, quote = quote, dec =
3: file(file, "rt")

Selection:
```

The `recover()` function will first print out the function call stack when an error occurrs. Then, you can choose to jump around the call stack and investigate the problem. When you choose a frame number, you will be put in the browser (just like the interactive debugger triggered with `debug()`) and will have the ability to poke around.

20.7 Summary

- There are three main indications of a problem/condition: `message`, `warning`, `error`; only an error is fatal
- When analyzing a function with a problem, make sure you can reproduce the problem, clearly state your expectations and how the output differs from your expectation
- Interactive debugging tools `traceback`, `debug`, `browser`, `trace`, and `recover` can be used to find problematic code in functions
- Debugging tools are not a substitute for thinking!

21. Profiling R Code

> Let's solve the problem but let's not make it worse by guessing. —*Gene Kranz, Apollo 13 Lead Flight Director*

Watch a video of this section[1]

R comes with a profiler to help you optimize your code and improve its performance. In generall, it's usually a bad idea to focus on optimizing your code at the very beginning of development. Rather, in the beginning it's better to focus on translating your ideas into code and writing code that's coherent and readable. The problem is that heavily optimized code tends to be obscure and difficult to read, making it harder to debug and revise. Better to get all the bugs out first, then focus on optimizing.

Of course, when it comes to optimizing code, the question is what should you optimize? Well, clearly should optimize the parts of your code that are running slowly, but how do we know what parts those are?

This is what the profiler is for. Profiling is a systematic way to examine how much time is spent in different parts of a program.

Sometimes profiling becomes necessary as a project grows and layers of code are placed on top of each other. Often you might write some code that runs fine once. But then later, you might put that same code in a big loop that runs 1,000 times. Now the original code that took 1 second to run is taking 1,000 seconds to run! Getting that little piece of original code to run faster will help the entire loop.

It's tempting to think you just *know* where the bottlenecks in your code are. I mean, after all, you write it! But trust me, I can't tell you how many times I've been surprised at where exactly my code is spending all its time. The reality is that *profiling is better than guessing*. Better to collect some data than to go on hunches alone. Ultimately, getting the biggest impact on speeding up code depends on knowing where the code spends most of its time. This cannot be done without some sort of rigorous performance analysis or profiling.

> We should forget about small efficiencies, say about 97% of the time: premature optimization is the root of all evil —*Donald Knuth*

The basic principles of optimizing your code are:

- Design first, then optimize
- Remember: Premature optimization is the root of all evil
- Measure (collect data), don't guess.
- If you're going to be scientist, you need to apply the same principles here!

---
[1] https://youtu.be/pHFgb12uG5s

21.1 Using `system.time()`

They `system.time()` function takes an arbitrary R expression as input (can be wrapped in curly braces) and returns the amount of time taken to evaluate the expression. The `system.time()` function computes the time (in seconds) needed to execute an expression and if there's an error, gives the time until the error occurred. The function returns an object of class `proc_time` which contains two useful bits of information:

- *user time*: time charged to the CPU(s) for this expression
- *elapsed time*: "wall clock" time, the amount of time that passes for *you* as you're sitting there

Usually, the user time and elapsed time are relatively close, for straight computing tasks. But there are a few situations where the two can diverge, sometimes dramatically. The elapsed time may be *greater than* the user time if the CPU spends a lot of time waiting around. This commonly happens if your R expression involes some input or output, which depends on the activity of the file system and the disk (or the Internet, if using a network connection).

The elapsed time may be *smaller than* the user time if your machine has multiple cores/processors (and is capable of using them). For example, multi-threaded BLAS libraries (vecLib/Accelerate, ATLAS, ACML, MKL) can greatly speed up linear algebra calculations and are commonly installed on even desktop systems these days. Also, parallel processing done via something like the `parallell` package can make the elapsed time smaller than the user time. When you have multiple processors/-cores/machines working in parallel, the amount of time that the collection of CPUs spends working on a problem is the same as with a single CPU, but because they are operating in parallel, there is a savings in elapsed time.

Here's an example of where the elapsed time is greater than the user time.

```
## Elapsed time > user time
system.time(readLines("http://www.jhsph.edu"))
   user  system elapsed
  0.004   0.002   0.431
```

Most of the time in this expression is spent waiting for the connection to the web server and waiting for the data to travel back to my computer. This doesn't involve the CPU and so the CPU simply waits around for things to get done. Hence, the user time is small.

In this example, the elapsed time is smaller than the user time.

```
## Elapsed time < user time
> hilbert <- function(n) {
+         i <- 1:n
+         1 / outer(i - 1, i, "+")
+ }
> x <- hilbert(1000)
> system.time(svd(x))
   user  system elapsed
  1.035   0.255   0.462
```

In this case I ran a singular value decomposition on the matrix in x, which is a common linear algebra procedure. Because my computer is able to split the work across multiple processors, the elapsed time is about half the user time.

21.2 Timing Longer Expressions

You can time longer expressions by wrapping them in curly braces within the call to system.time().

```
> system.time({
+         n <- 1000
+         r <- numeric(n)
+         for(i in 1:n) {
+                 x <- rnorm(n)
+                 r[i] <- mean(x)
+         }
+ })
   user  system elapsed
  0.081   0.004   0.088
```

If your expression is getting pretty long (more than 2 or 3 lines), it might be better to either break it into smaller pieces or to use the profiler. The problem is that if the expression is too long, you won't be able to identify which part of the code is causing the bottleneck.

21.3 The R Profiler

Watch a video of this section[2]

Using system.time() allows you to test certain functions or code blocks to see if they are taking excessive amounts of time. However, this approach assumes that you already know where the problem is and can call system.time() on it that piece of code. What if you don't know where to start?

---

[2]https://youtu.be/BZVcMPtlJ4A

This is where the profiler comes in handy. The `Rprof()` function starts the profiler in R. Note that R must be compiled with profiler support (but this is usually the case). In conjunction with `Rprof()`, we will use the `summaryRprof()` function which summarizes the output from `Rprof()` (otherwise it's not really readable). Note that you should NOT use `system.time()` and `Rprof()` together, or you will be sad.

`Rprof()` keeps track of the function call stack at regularly sampled intervals and tabulates how much time is spent inside each function. By default, the profiler samples the function call stack every 0.02 seconds. This means that if your code runs very quickly (say, under 0.02 seconds), the profiler is not useful. But of your code runs that fast, you probably don't need the profiler.

The profiler is started by calling the `Rprof()` function.

```
> Rprof()      ## Turn on the profiler
```

You don't need any other arguments. By default it will write its output to a file called `Rprof.out`. You can specify the name of the output file if you don't want to use this default.

Once you call the `Rprof()` function, everything that you do from then on will be measured by the profiler. Therefore, you usually only want to run a single R function or expression once you turn on the profiler and then immediately turn it off. The reason is that if you mix too many function calls together when running the profiler, all of the results will be mixed together and you won't be able to sort out where the bottlenecks are. In reality, I usually only run a single function with the profiler on.

The profiler can be turned off by passing `NULL` to `Rprof()`.

```
> Rprof(NULL)     ## Turn off the profiler
```

The raw output from the profiler looks something like this. Here I'm calling the `lm()` function on some data with the profiler running.

```
## lm(y ~ x)

sample.interval=10000
"list" "eval" "eval" "model.frame.default" "model.frame" "eval" "eval" "lm"
"list" "eval" "eval" "model.frame.default" "model.frame" "eval" "eval" "lm"
"list" "eval" "eval" "model.frame.default" "model.frame" "eval" "eval" "lm"
"list" "eval" "eval" "model.frame.default" "model.frame" "eval" "eval" "lm"
"na.omit" "model.frame.default" "model.frame" "eval" "eval" "lm"
"na.omit" "model.frame.default" "model.frame" "eval" "eval" "lm"
"na.omit" "model.frame.default" "model.frame" "eval" "eval" "lm"
"na.omit" "model.frame.default" "model.frame" "eval" "eval" "lm"
"na.omit" "model.frame.default" "model.frame" "eval" "eval" "lm"
"na.omit" "model.frame.default" "model.frame" "eval" "eval" "lm"
```

```
"na.omit" "model.frame.default" "model.frame" "eval" "eval" "lm"
"lm.fit" "lm"
"lm.fit" "lm"
"lm.fit" "lm"
```

At each line of the output, the profiler writes out the function call stack. For example, on the very first line of the output you can see that the code is 8 levels deep in the call stack. This is where you need the `summaryRprof()` function to help you interpret this data.

21.4 Using `summaryRprof()`

The `summaryRprof()` function tabulates the R profiler output and calculates how much time is spent in which function. There are two methods for normalizing the data.

- "by.total" divides the time spend in each function by the total run time
- "by.self" does the same as "by.total" but first subtracts out time spent in functions above the current function in the call stack. I personally find this output to be much more useful.

Here is what `summaryRprof()` reports in the "by.total" output.

```
$by.total
                        total.time total.pct self.time self.pct
"lm"                          7.41    100.00      0.30     4.05
"lm.fit"                      3.50     47.23      2.99    40.35
"model.frame.default"         2.24     30.23      0.12     1.62
"eval"                        2.24     30.23      0.00     0.00
"model.frame"                 2.24     30.23      0.00     0.00
"na.omit"                     1.54     20.78      0.24     3.24
"na.omit.data.frame"          1.30     17.54      0.49     6.61
"lapply"                      1.04     14.04      0.00     0.00
"[.data.frame"                1.03     13.90      0.79    10.66
"["                           1.03     13.90      0.00     0.00
"as.list.data.frame"          0.82     11.07      0.82    11.07
"as.list"                     0.82     11.07      0.00     0.00
```

Because `lm()` is the function that I called from the command line, of course 100% of the time is spent somewhere in that function. However, what this doesn't show is that if `lm()` immediately calls another function (like `lm.fit()`, which does most of the heavy lifting), then in reality, most of the time is spent in *that* function, rather than in the top-level `lm()` function.

The "by.self" output corrects for this discrepancy.

```
$by.self
                       self.time self.pct total.time total.pct
"lm.fit"                   2.99    40.35      3.50     47.23
"as.list.data.frame"       0.82    11.07      0.82     11.07
"[.data.frame"             0.79    10.66      1.03     13.90
"structure"                0.73     9.85      0.73      9.85
"na.omit.data.frame"       0.49     6.61      1.30     17.54
"list"                     0.46     6.21      0.46      6.21
"lm"                       0.30     4.05      7.41    100.00
"model.matrix.default"     0.27     3.64      0.79     10.66
"na.omit"                  0.24     3.24      1.54     20.78
"as.character"             0.18     2.43      0.18      2.43
"model.frame.default"      0.12     1.62      2.24     30.23
"anyDuplicated.default"    0.02     0.27      0.02      0.27
```

Now you can see that only about 4% of the runtime is spent in the actual lm() function, whereas over 40% of the time is spent in lm.fit(). In this case, this is no surprise since the lm.fit() function is the function that actually fits the linear model.

You can see that a reasonable amount of time is spent in functions not necessarily associated with linear modeling (i.e. as.list.data.frame, [.data.frame). This is because the lm() function does a bit of pre-processing and checking before it actually fits the model. This is common with modeling functions—the preprocessing and checking is useful to see if there are any errors. But those two functions take up over 1.5 seconds of runtime. What if you want to fit this model 10,000 times? You're going to be spending a lot of time in preprocessing and checking.

The final bit of output that summaryRprof() provides is the sampling interval and the total runtime.

```
$sample.interval
[1] 0.02

$sampling.time
[1] 7.41
```

21.5 Summary

- Rprof() runs the profiler for performance of analysis of R code
- summaryRprof() summarizes the output of Rprof() and gives percent of time spent in each function (with two types of normalization)
- Good to break your code into functions so that the profiler can give useful information about where time is being spent
- C or Fortran code is not profiled

22. Simulation

22.1 Generating Random Numbers

Watch a video of this section[1]

Simulation is an important (and big) topic for both statistics and for a variety of other areas where there is a need to introduce randomness. Sometimes you want to implement a statistical procedure that requires random number generation or sampling (i.e. Markov chain Monte Carlo, the bootstrap, random forests, bagging) and sometimes you want to simulate a system and random number generators can be used to model random inputs.

R comes with a set of pseudo-random number generators that allow you to simulate from well-known probability distributions like the Normal, Poisson, and binomial. Some example functions for probability distributions in R

- `rnorm`: generate random Normal variates with a given mean and standard deviation
- `dnorm`: evaluate the Normal probability density (with a given mean/SD) at a point (or vector of points)
- `pnorm`: evaluate the cumulative distribution function for a Normal distribution
- `rpois`: generate random Poisson variates with a given rate

For each probability distribution there are typically four functions available that start with a "r", "d", "p", and "q". The "r" function is the one that actually simulates randon numbers from that distribution. The other functions are prefixed with a

- d for density
- r for random number generation
- p for cumulative distribution
- q for quantile function (inverse cumulative distribution)

If you're only interested in simulating random numbers, then you will likely only need the "r" functions and not the others. However, if you intend to simulate from arbitrary probability distributions using something like rejection sampling, then you will need the other functions too.

Probably the most common probability distribution to work with the is the Normal distribution (also known as the Gaussian). Working with the Normal distributions requires using these four functions

---

[1]https://youtu.be/tzz4flrajr0

```
dnorm(x, mean = 0, sd = 1, log = FALSE)
pnorm(q, mean = 0, sd = 1, lower.tail = TRUE, log.p = FALSE)
qnorm(p, mean = 0, sd = 1, lower.tail = TRUE, log.p = FALSE)
rnorm(n, mean = 0, sd = 1)
```

Here we simulate standard Normal random numbers with mean 0 and standard deviation 1.

```
> ## Simulate standard Normal random numbers
> x <- rnorm(10)
> x
 [1]  0.01874617 -0.18425254 -1.37133055 -0.59916772  0.29454513
 [6]  0.38979430 -1.20807618 -0.36367602 -1.62667268 -0.25647839
```

We can modify the default parameters to simulate numbers with mean 20 and standard deviation 2.

```
> x <- rnorm(10, 20, 2)
> x
 [1] 22.20356 21.51156 19.52353 21.97489 21.48278 20.17869 18.09011
 [8] 19.60970 21.85104 20.96596
> summary(x)
   Min. 1st Qu.  Median    Mean 3rd Qu.    Max.
  18.09   19.75   21.22   20.74   21.77   22.20
```

If you wanted to know what was the probability of a random Normal variable of being less than, say, 2, you could use the `pnorm()` function to do that calculation.

```
> pnorm(2)
[1] 0.9772499
```

You never know when that calculation will come in handy.

22.2 Setting the random number seed

When simulating any random numbers it is essential to set the *random number seed*. Setting the random number seed with `set.seed()` ensures reproducibility of the sequence of random numbers.

For example, I can generate 5 Normal random numbers with `rnorm()`.

```
> set.seed(1)
> rnorm(5)
[1] -0.6264538  0.1836433 -0.8356286  1.5952808  0.3295078
```

Note that if I call `rnorm()` again I will of course get a different set of 5 random numbers.

```
> rnorm(5)
[1] -0.8204684  0.4874291  0.7383247  0.5757814 -0.3053884
```

If I want to reproduce the original set of random numbers, I can just reset the seed with `set.seed()`.

```
> set.seed(1)
> rnorm(5)         ## Same as before
[1] -0.6264538  0.1836433 -0.8356286  1.5952808  0.3295078
```

In general, you should **always set the random number seed when conducting a simulation!** Otherwise, you will not be able to reconstruct the exact numbers that you produced in an analysis.

It is possible to generate random numbers from other probability distributions like the Poisson. The Poisson distribution is commonly used to model data that come in the form of counts.

```
> rpois(10, 1)      ## Counts with a mean of 1
 [1] 0 0 1 1 2 1 1 4 1 2
> rpois(10, 2)      ## Counts with a mean of 2
 [1] 4 1 2 0 1 1 0 1 4 1
> rpois(10, 20)     ## Counts with a mean of 20
 [1] 19 19 24 23 22 24 23 20 11 22
```

22.3 Simulating a Linear Model

Watch a video of this section[2]

Simulating random numbers is useful but sometimes we want to simulate values that come from a specific *model*. For that we need to specify the model and then simulate from it using the functions described above.

Suppose we want to simulate from the following linear model

$$y = \beta_0 + \beta_1 x + \varepsilon$$

where $\varepsilon \sim \mathcal{N}(0, 2^2)$. Assume $x \sim \mathcal{N}(0, 1^2)$, $\beta_0 = 0.5$ and $\beta_1 = 2$. The variable x might represent an important predictor of the outcome y. Here's how we could do that in R.

---
[2]https://youtu.be/p7kSSSsv4ms

```
> ## Always set your seed!
> set.seed(20)
> 
> ## Simulate predictor variable
> x <- rnorm(100)
> 
> ## Simulate the error term
> e <- rnorm(100, 0, 2)
> 
> ## Compute the outcome via the model
> y <- 0.5 + 2 * x + e
> summary(y)
   Min. 1st Qu.  Median    Mean 3rd Qu.    Max.
-6.4080 -1.5400  0.6789  0.6893  2.9300  6.5050
```

We can plot the results of the model simulation.

```
> plot(x, y)
```

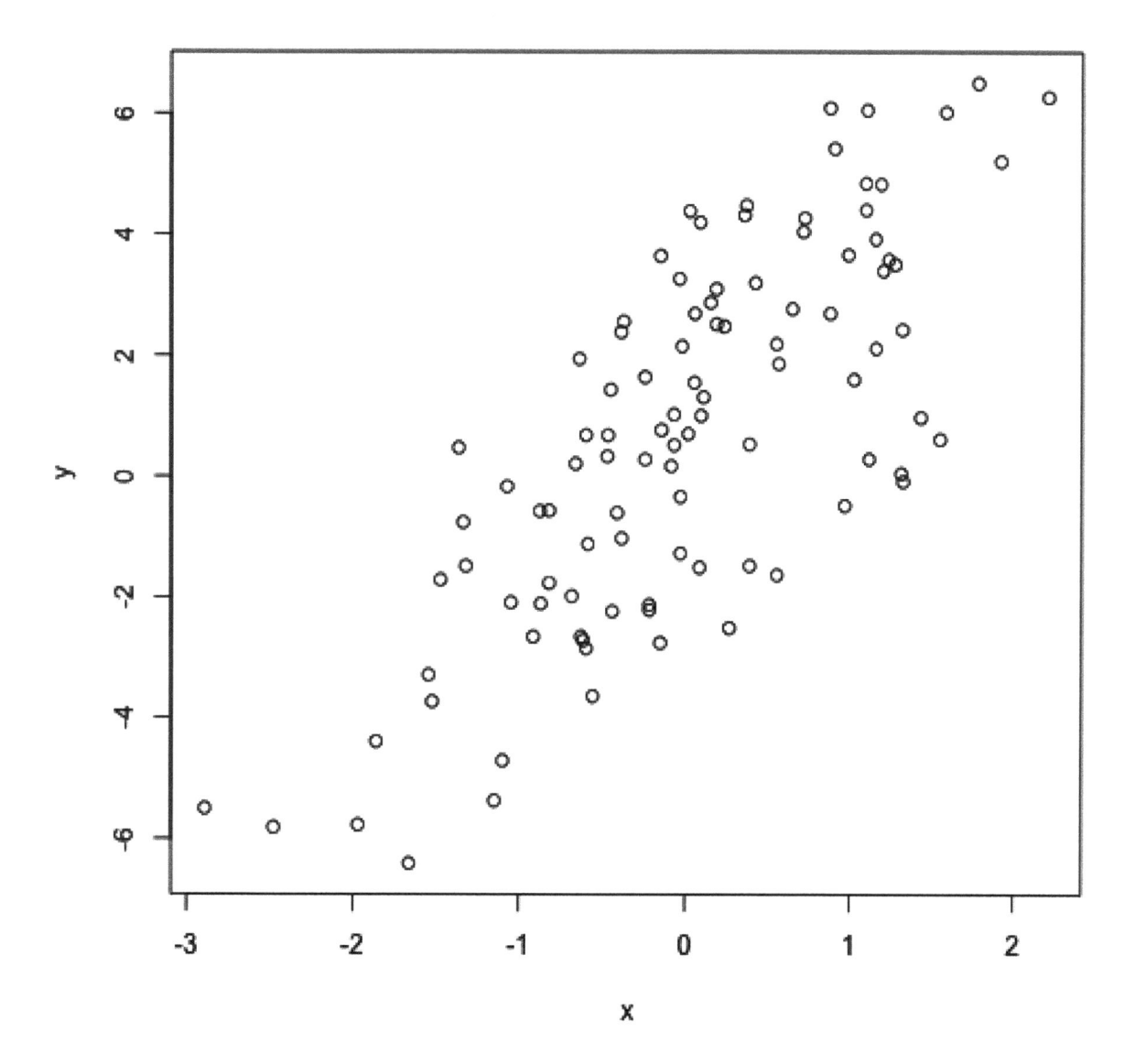

plot of chunk Linear Model

What if we wanted to simulate a predictor variable x that is binary instead of having a Normal distribution. We can use the rbinom() function to simulate binary random variables.

```
> set.seed(10)
> x <- rbinom(100, 1, 0.5)
> str(x)      ## 'x' is now 0s and 1s
 int [1:100] 1 0 0 1 0 0 0 0 1 0 ...
```

Then we can procede with the rest of the model as before.

```
> e <- rnorm(100, 0, 2)
> y <- 0.5 + 2 * x + e
> plot(x, y)
```

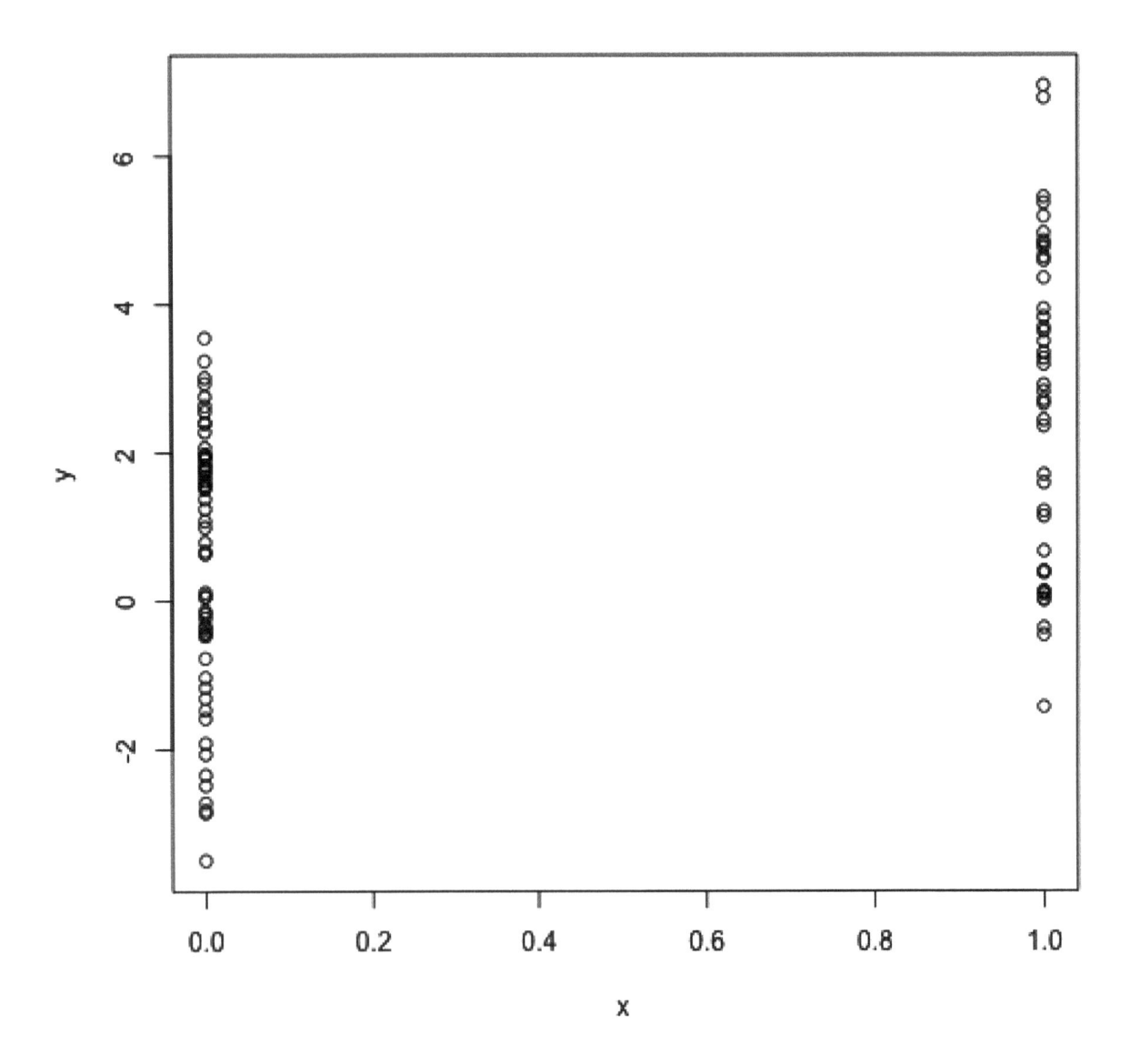

plot of chunk Linear Model Binary

We can also simulate from *generalized linear model* where the errors are no longer from a Normal distribution but come from some other distribution. For examples, suppose we want to simulate from a Poisson log-linear model where

$$Y \sim Poisson(\mu)$$

$$\log \mu = \beta_0 + \beta_1 x$$

and $\beta_0 = 0.5$ and $\beta_1 = 0.3$. We need to use the `rpois()` function for this

```
> set.seed(1)
>
> ## Simulate the predictor variable as before
> x <- rnorm(100)
```

Now we need to compute the log mean of the model and then exponentiate it to get the mean to pass to `rpois()`.

```
> log.mu <- 0.5 + 0.3 * x
> y <- rpois(100, exp(log.mu))
> summary(y)
   Min. 1st Qu.  Median    Mean 3rd Qu.    Max.
   0.00    1.00    1.00    1.55    2.00    6.00
> plot(x, y)
```

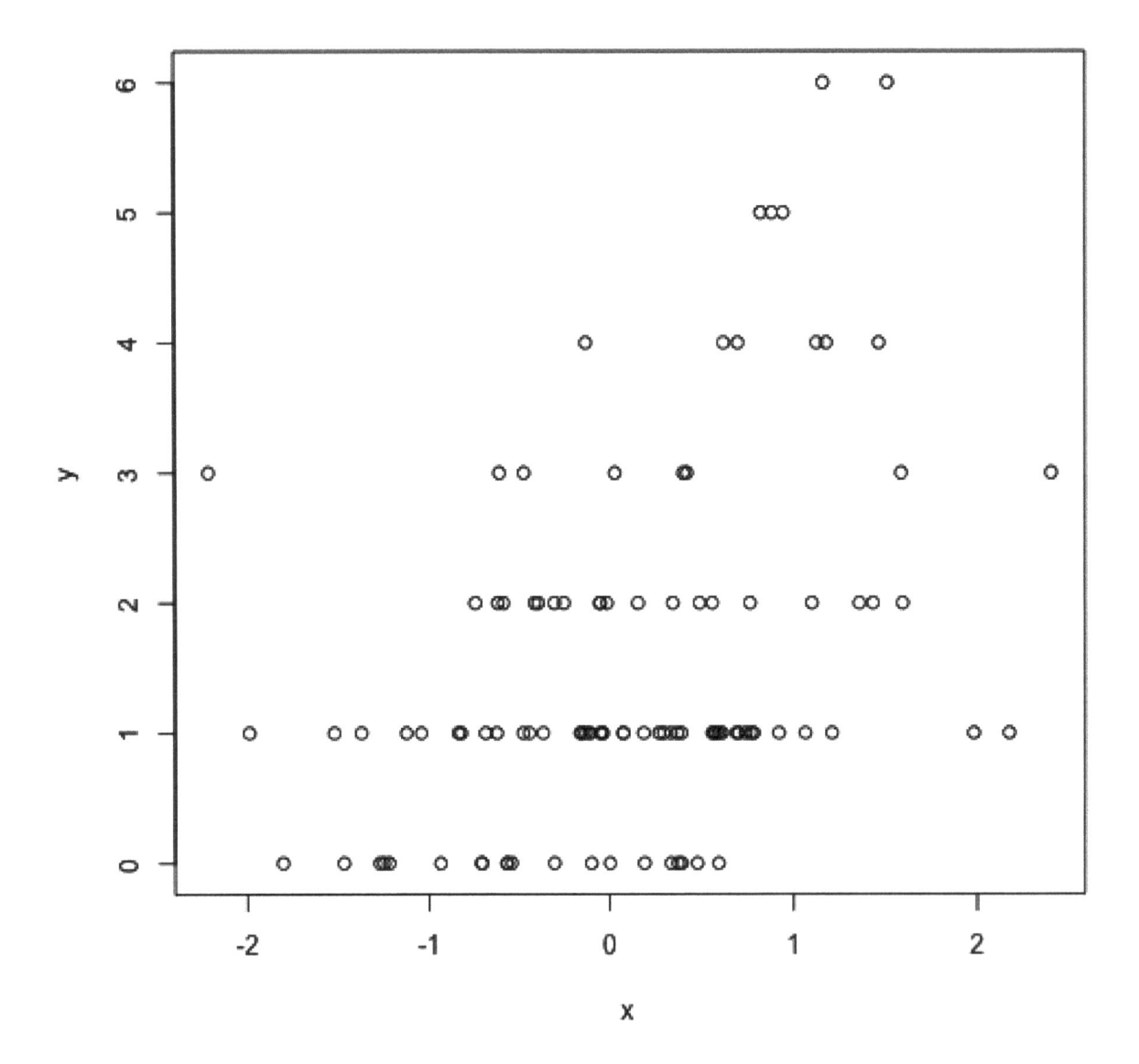

plot of chunk Poisson Log-Linear Model

You can build arbitrarily complex models like this by simulating more predictors or making transformations of those predictors (e.g. squaring, log transformations, etc.).

22.4 Random Sampling

Watch a video of this section[3]

---
[3]https://youtu.be/-7GA10KWDJg

The `sample()` function draws randomly from a specified set of (scalar) objects allowing you to sample from arbitrary distributions of numbers.

```
> set.seed(1)
> sample(1:10, 4)
[1] 3 4 5 7
> sample(1:10, 4)
[1] 3 9 8 5
>
> ## Doesn't have to be numbers
> sample(letters, 5)
[1] "q" "b" "e" "x" "p"
>
> ## Do a random permutation
> sample(1:10)
 [1]  4  7 10  6  9  2  8  3  1  5
> sample(1:10)
 [1]  2  3  4  1  9  5 10  8  6  7
>
> ## Sample w/replacement
> sample(1:10, replace = TRUE)
 [1] 2 9 7 8 2 8 5 9 7 8
```

To sample more complicated things, such as rows from a data frame or a list, you can sample the indices into an object rather than the elements of the object itself.

Here's how you can sample rows from a data frame.

```
> library(datasets)
> data(airquality)
> head(airquality)
  Ozone Solar.R Wind Temp Month Day
1    41     190  7.4   67     5   1
2    36     118  8.0   72     5   2
3    12     149 12.6   74     5   3
4    18     313 11.5   62     5   4
5    NA      NA 14.3   56     5   5
6    28      NA 14.9   66     5   6
```

Now we just need to create the index vector indexing the rows of the data frame and sample directly from that index vector.

```
> set.seed(20)
> 
> ## Create index vector
> idx <- seq_len(nrow(airquality))
> 
> ## Sample from the index vector
> samp <- sample(idx, 6)
> airquality[samp, ]
    Ozone Solar.R Wind Temp Month Day
135    21     259 15.5   76     9  12
117   168     238  3.4   81     8  25
43     NA     250  9.2   92     6  12
80     79     187  5.1   87     7  19
144    13     238 12.6   64     9  21
146    36     139 10.3   81     9  23
```

Other more complex objects can be sampled in this way, as long as there's a way to index the sub-elements of the object.

22.5 Summary

- Drawing samples from specific probability distributions can be done with "r" functions
- Standard distributions are built in: Normal, Poisson, Binomial, Exponential, Gamma, etc.
- The `sample()` function can be used to draw random samples from arbitrary vectors
- Setting the random number generator seed via `set.seed()` is critical for reproducibility

23. Data Analysis Case Study: Changes in Fine Particle Air Pollution in the U.S.

This chapter presents an example data analysis looking at changes in fine particulate matter (PM) air pollution in the United States using the Environmental Protection Agencies freely available national monitoring data. The purpose of the chapter is to just show how the various tools that we have covered in this book can be used to read, manipulate, and summarize data so that you can develop statistical evidence for relevant real-world questions.

Watch a video of this chapter[1]

23.1 Synopsis

In this chapter we aim to describe the changes in fine particle (PM2.5) outdoor air pollution in the United States between the years 1999 and 2012. Our overall hypothesis is that outdoor PM2.5 has decreased on average across the U.S. due to nationwide regulatory requirements arising from the Clean Air Act. To investigate this hypothesis, we obtained PM2.5 data from the U.S. Environmental Protection Agency which is collected from monitors sited across the U.S. We specifically obtained data for the years 1999 and 2012 (the most recent complete year available). From these data, we found that, on average across the U.S., levels of PM2.5 have decreased between 1999 and 2012. At one individual monitor, we found that levels have decreased and that the variability of PM2.5 has decreased. Most individual states also experienced decreases in PM2.5, although some states saw increases.

23.2 Loading and Processing the Raw Data

From the EPA Air Quality System[2] we obtained data on fine particulate matter air pollution (PM2.5) that is monitored across the U.S. as part of the nationwide PM monitoring network. We obtained the files for the years 1999 and 2012.

---
[1]https://youtu.be/VE-6bQvyfTQ
[2]http://aqsdr1.epa.gov/aqsweb/aqstmp/airdata/download_files.html

158   Data Analysis Case Study: Changes in Fine Particle Air Pollution in the U.S.

Reading in the 1999 data

We first read in the 1999 data from the raw text file included in the zip archive. The data is a delimited file were fields are delimited with the | character and missing values are coded as blank fields. We skip some commented lines in the beginning of the file and initially we do not read the header data.

```
> pm0 <- read.table("pm25_data/RD_501_88101_1999-0.txt", comment.char = "#", header = FALS\
E, sep = "|", na.strings = "")
```

After reading in the 1999 we check the first few rows (there are 117,421) rows in this dataset.

```
> dim(pm0)
[1] 117421     28
> head(pm0[, 1:13])
  V1 V2 V3 V4 V5    V6 V7 V8  V9 V10      V11   V12    V13
1 RD  I  1 27  1 88101  1  7 105 120 19990103 00:00     NA
2 RD  I  1 27  1 88101  1  7 105 120 19990106 00:00     NA
3 RD  I  1 27  1 88101  1  7 105 120 19990109 00:00     NA
4 RD  I  1 27  1 88101  1  7 105 120 19990112 00:00  8.841
5 RD  I  1 27  1 88101  1  7 105 120 19990115 00:00 14.920
6 RD  I  1 27  1 88101  1  7 105 120 19990118 00:00  3.878
```

We then attach the column headers to the dataset and make sure that they are properly formated for R data frames.

```
> cnames <- readLines("pm25_data/RD_501_88101_1999-0.txt", 1)
> cnames <- strsplit(cnames, "|", fixed = TRUE)
> ## Ensure names are properly formatted
> names(pm0) <- make.names(cnames[[1]])
> head(pm0[, 1:13])
  X..RD Action.Code State.Code County.Code Site.ID Parameter POC
1    RD           I          1          27       1     88101   1
2    RD           I          1          27       1     88101   1
3    RD           I          1          27       1     88101   1
4    RD           I          1          27       1     88101   1
5    RD           I          1          27       1     88101   1
6    RD           I          1          27       1     88101   1
  Sample.Duration Unit Method     Date Start.Time Sample.Value
1               7  105    120 19990103      00:00           NA
2               7  105    120 19990106      00:00           NA
3               7  105    120 19990109      00:00           NA
4               7  105    120 19990112      00:00        8.841
5               7  105    120 19990115      00:00       14.920
6               7  105    120 19990118      00:00        3.878
```

The column we are interested in is the `Sample.Value` column which contains the PM2.5 measurements. Here we extract that column and print a brief summary.

```
> x0 <- pm0$Sample.Value
> summary(x0)
   Min. 1st Qu.  Median    Mean 3rd Qu.    Max.    NA's
   0.00    7.20   11.50   13.74   17.90  157.10   13217
```

Missing values are a common problem with environmental data and so we check to se what proportion of the observations are missing (i.e. coded as NA).

```
> mean(is.na(x0))   ## Are missing values important here?
[1] 0.1125608
```

Because the proportion of missing values is relatively low (0.1125608), we choose to ignore missing values for now.

Reading in the 2012 data

We then read in the 2012 data in the same manner in which we read the 1999 data (the data files are in the same format).

```
> pm1 <- read.table("pm25_data/RD_501_88101_2012-0.txt", comment.char = "#",
+                   header = FALSE, sep = "|", na.strings = "", nrow = 1304290)
```

We also set the column names (they are the same as the 1999 dataset) and extract the `Sample.Value` column from this dataset.

```
> names(pm1) <- make.names(cnames[[1]])
> x1 <- pm1$Sample.Value
```

23.3 Results

Entire U.S. analysis

In order to show aggregate changes in PM across the entire monitoring network, we can make boxplots of all monitor values in 1999 and 2012. Here, we take the log of the PM values to adjust for the skew in the data.

```
> boxplot(log2(x0), log2(x1))
Warning in boxplot.default(log2(x0), log2(x1)): NaNs produced
Warning in bplt(at[i], wid = width[i], stats = z$stats[, i], out = z$out[z
$group == : Outlier (-Inf) in boxplot 1 is not drawn
Warning in bplt(at[i], wid = width[i], stats = z$stats[, i], out = z$out[z
$group == : Outlier (-Inf) in boxplot 2 is not drawn
```

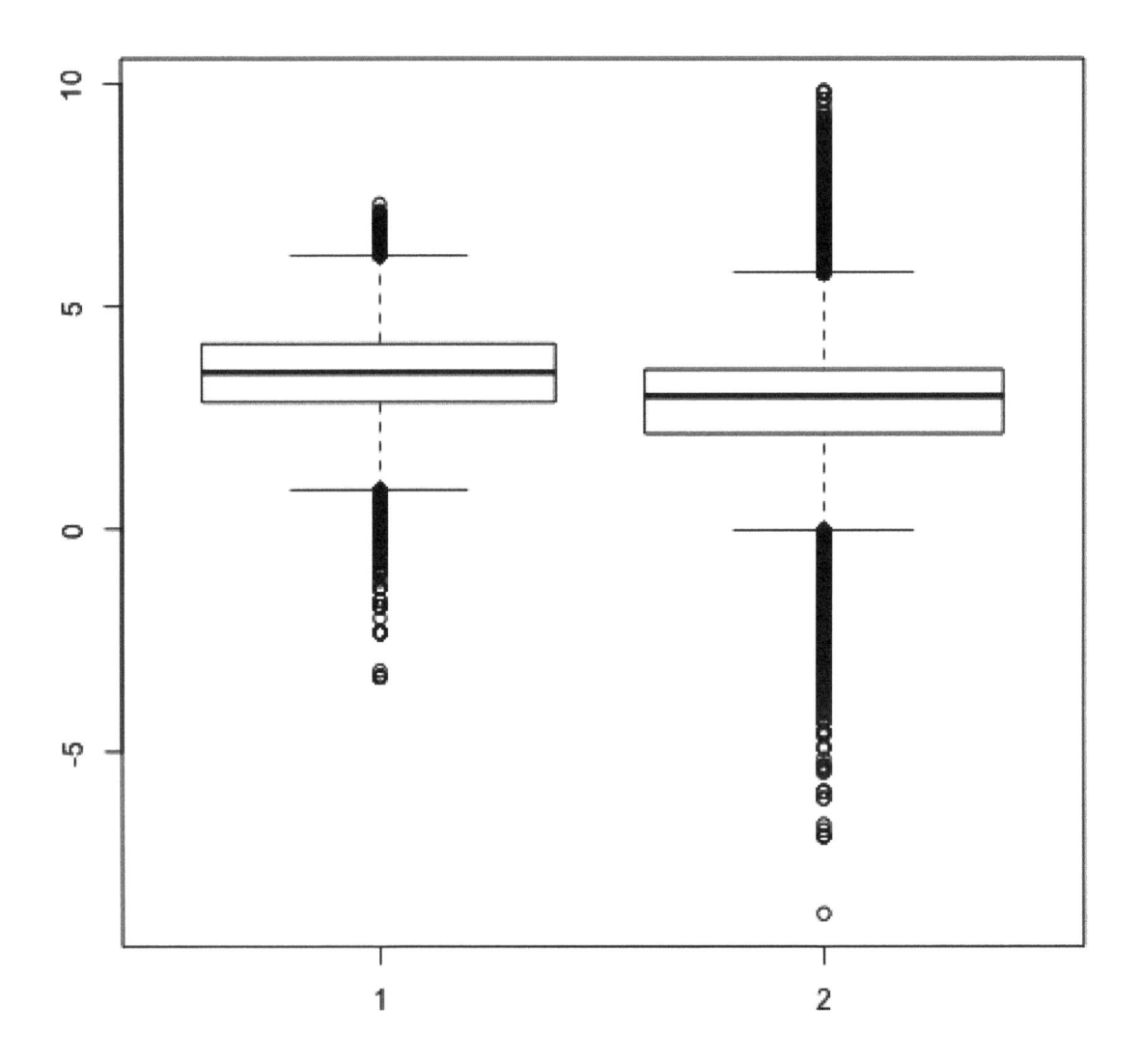

plot of chunk boxplot log values

```
> summary(x0)
   Min. 1st Qu.  Median    Mean 3rd Qu.    Max.    NA's
   0.00    7.20   11.50   13.74   17.90  157.10   13217
> summary(x1)
   Min. 1st Qu.  Median    Mean 3rd Qu.    Max.    NA's
 -10.00    4.00    7.63    9.14   12.00  909.00   73133
```

Interestingly, from the summary of `x1` it appears there are some negative values of PM, which in general should not occur. We can investigate that somewhat to see if there is anything we should worry about.

```
> negative <- x1 < 0
> mean(negative, na.rm = T)
[1] 0.0215034
```

There is a relatively small proportion of values that are negative, which is perhaps reassuring. In order to investigate this a step further we can extract the date of each measurement from the original data frame. The idea here is that perhaps negative values occur more often in some parts of the year than other parts. However, the original data are formatted as character strings so we convert them to R's `Date` format for easier manipulation.

```
> dates <- pm1$Date
> dates <- as.Date(as.character(dates), "%Y%m%d")
```

We can then extract the month from each of the dates with negative values and attempt to identify when negative values occur most often.

```
> missing.months <- month.name[as.POSIXlt(dates)$mon + 1]
> tab <- table(factor(missing.months, levels = month.name))
> round(100 * tab / sum(tab))

  January  February     March     April       May      June      July
       15        13        15        13        14        13         8
   August September   October  November  December
        6         3         0         0         0
```

From the table above it appears that bulk of the negative values occur in the first six months of the year (January–June). However, beyond that simple observation, it is not clear why the negative values occur. That said, given the relatively low proportion of negative values, we will ignore them for now.

Changes in PM levels at an individual monitor

So far we have examined the change in PM levels on average across the country. One issue with the previous analysis is that the monitoring network could have changed in the time period between 1999 and 2012. So if for some reason in 2012 there are more monitors concentrated in cleaner parts of the country than there were in 1999, it might appear the PM levels decreased when in fact they didn't. In this section we will focus on a single monitor in New York State to see if PM levels *at that monitor* decreased from 1999 to 2012.

Our first task is to identify a monitor in New York State that has data in 1999 and 2012 (not all monitors operated during both time periods). First we subset the data frames to only include data from New York (State.Code == 36) and only include the County.Code and the Site.ID (i.e. monitor number) variables.

```
> site0 <- unique(subset(pm0, State.Code == 36, c(County.Code, Site.ID)))
> site1 <- unique(subset(pm1, State.Code == 36, c(County.Code, Site.ID)))
```

Then we create a new variable that combines the county code and the site ID into a single string.

```
> site0 <- paste(site0[,1], site0[,2], sep = ".")
> site1 <- paste(site1[,1], site1[,2], sep = ".")
> str(site0)
 chr [1:33] "1.5" "1.12" "5.73" "5.80" "5.83" "5.110" ...
> str(site1)
 chr [1:18] "1.5" "1.12" "5.80" "5.133" "13.11" "29.5" ...
```

Finaly, we want the intersection between the sites present in 1999 and 2012 so that we might choose a monitor that has data in both periods.

```
> both <- intersect(site0, site1)
> print(both)
 [1] "1.5"     "1.12"    "5.80"    "13.11"   "29.5"    "31.3"    "63.2008"
 [8] "67.1015" "85.55"   "101.3"
```

Here (above) we can see that there are 10 monitors that were operating in both time periods. However, rather than choose one at random, it might best to choose one that had a reasonable amount of data in each year.

```
> ## Find how many observations available at each monitor
> pm0$county.site <- with(pm0, paste(County.Code, Site.ID, sep = "."))
> pm1$county.site <- with(pm1, paste(County.Code, Site.ID, sep = "."))
> cnt0 <- subset(pm0, State.Code == 36 & county.site %in% both)
> cnt1 <- subset(pm1, State.Code == 36 & county.site %in% both)
```

Now that we have subsetted the original data frames to only include the data from the monitors that overlap between 1999 and 2012, we can split the data frames and count the number of observations at each monitor to see which ones have the most observations.

```
> ## 1999
> sapply(split(cnt0, cnt0$county.site), nrow)
    1.12     1.5   101.3   13.11    29.5    31.3    5.80 63.2008 67.1015
      61     122     152      61      61     183      61     122     122
   85.55
       7
> ## 2012
> sapply(split(cnt1, cnt1$county.site), nrow)
    1.12     1.5   101.3   13.11    29.5    31.3    5.80 63.2008 67.1015
      31      64      31      31      33      15      31      30      31
   85.55
      31
```

A number of monitors seem suitable from the output, but we will focus here on County 63 and site ID 2008.

```
> both.county <- 63
> both.id <- 2008
>
> ## Choose county 63 and side ID 2008
> pm1sub <- subset(pm1, State.Code == 36 & County.Code == both.county & Site.ID == both.id)
> pm0sub <- subset(pm0, State.Code == 36 & County.Code == both.county & Site.ID == both.id)
```

Now we plot the time series data of PM for the monitor in both years.

```
> dates1 <- as.Date(as.character(pm1sub$Date), "%Y%m%d")
> x1sub <- pm1sub$Sample.Value
> dates0 <- as.Date(as.character(pm0sub$Date), "%Y%m%d")
> x0sub <- pm0sub$Sample.Value
>
> ## Find global range
> rng <- range(x0sub, x1sub, na.rm = T)
> par(mfrow = c(1, 2), mar = c(4, 5, 2, 1))
> plot(dates0, x0sub, pch = 20, ylim = rng, xlab = "", ylab = expression(PM[2.5] * " (" * \
mu * g/m^3 * ")"))
> abline(h = median(x0sub, na.rm = T))
> plot(dates1, x1sub, pch = 20, ylim = rng, xlab = "", ylab = expression(PM[2.5] * " (" * \
mu * g/m^3 * ")"))
> abline(h = median(x1sub, na.rm = T))
```

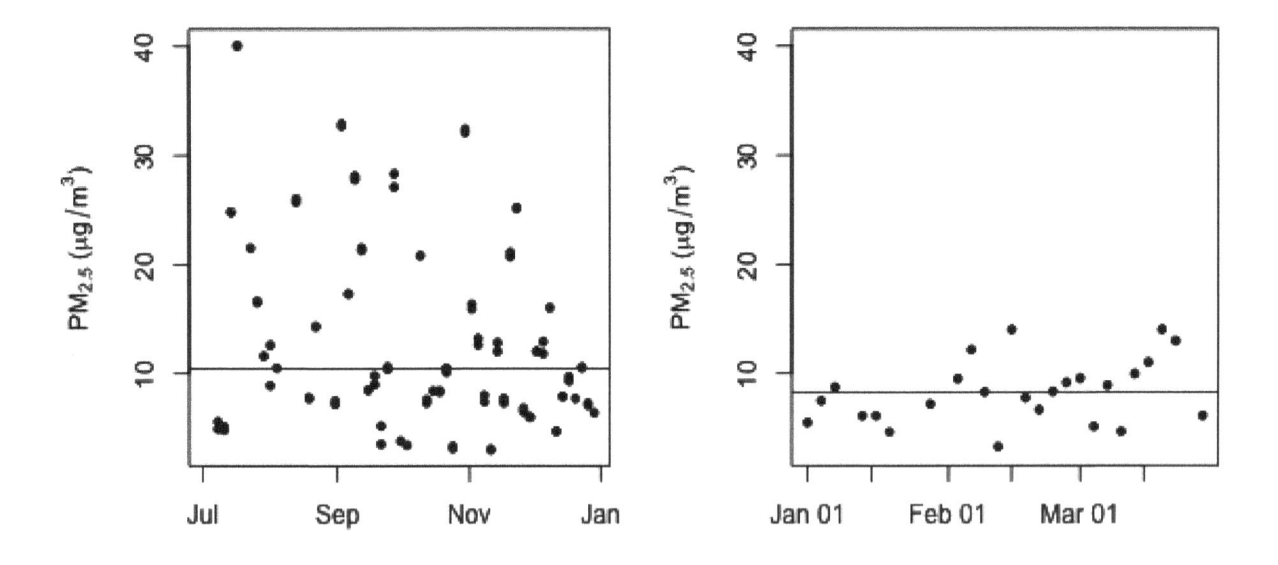

plot of chunk unnamed-chunk-11

From the plot above, we can that median levels of PM (horizontal solid line) have decreased a little from 10.45 in 1999 to 8.29 in 2012. However, perhaps more interesting is that the variation (spread) in the PM values in 2012 is much smaller than it was in 1999. This suggest that not only are median levels of PM lower in 2012, but that there are fewer large spikes from day to day. One issue with the data here is that the 1999 data are from July through December while the 2012 data are recorded in January through April. It would have been better if we'd had full-year data for both years as there could be some seasonal confounding going on.

Changes in state-wide PM levels

Although ambient air quality standards are set at the federal level in the U.S. and hence affect the entire country, the actual reduction and management of PM is left to the individual states. States that are not "in attainment" have to develop a plan to reduce PM so that that the are in attainment (eventually). Therefore, it might be useful to examine changes in PM at the state level. This analysis falls somewhere in between looking at the entire country all at once and looking at an individual monitor.

What we do here is calculate the mean of PM for each state in 1999 and 2012.

```
> ## 1999
> mn0 <- with(pm0, tapply(Sample.Value, State.Code, mean, na.rm = TRUE))
> ## 2012
> mn1 <- with(pm1, tapply(Sample.Value, State.Code, mean, na.rm = TRUE))
>
> ## Make separate data frames for states / years
> d0 <- data.frame(state = names(mn0), mean = mn0)
> d1 <- data.frame(state = names(mn1), mean = mn1)
> mrg <- merge(d0, d1, by = "state")
> head(mrg)
  state    mean.x    mean.y
1     1 19.956391 10.126190
2    10 14.492895 11.236059
3    11 15.786507 11.991697
4    12 11.137139  8.239690
5    13 19.943240 11.321364
6    15  4.861821  8.749336
```

Now make a plot that shows the 1999 state-wide means in one "column" and the 2012 state-wide means in another columns. We then draw a line connecting the means for each year in the same state to highlight the trend.

```
> par(mfrow = c(1, 1))
> rng <- range(mrg[,2], mrg[,3])
> with(mrg, plot(rep(1, 52), mrg[, 2], xlim = c(.5, 2.5), ylim = rng, xaxt = "n", xlab = "\
", ylab = "State-wide Mean PM"))
> with(mrg, points(rep(2, 52), mrg[, 3]))
> segments(rep(1, 52), mrg[, 2], rep(2, 52), mrg[, 3])
> axis(1, c(1, 2), c("1999", "2012"))
```

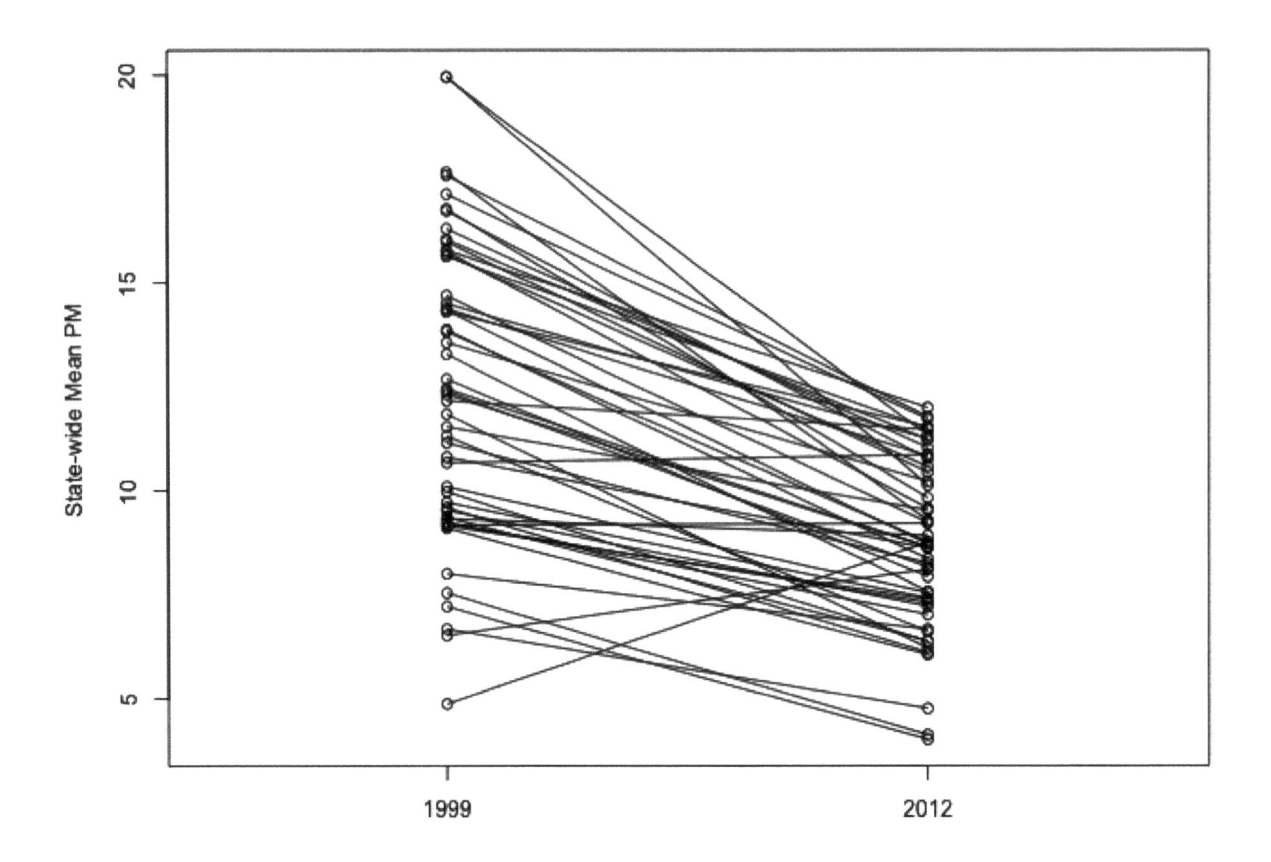

[plot: State-wide Mean PM in 1999 vs 2012]

From the plot above we can see that many states have decreased the average PM levels from 1999 to 2012 (although a few states actually increased their levels).

24. Parallel Computation

Many computations in R can be made faster by the use of parallel computation. Generally, parallel computation is the simultaneous execution of different pieces of a larger computation across multiple computing processors or cores. The basic idea is that if you can execute a computation in X seconds on a single processor, then you should be able to execute it in X/n seconds on n proessors. Such a speed-up is generally not possible because of overhead and various barriers to splitting up a problem into n pieces, but it is often possible to come close in simple problems.

It used to be that parallel computation was squarely in the domain of "high-performance computing", where expensive machines were linked together via high-speed networking to create large clusters of computers. In those kinds of settings, it was important to have sophisticated software to manage the communication of data between different computers in the cluster. Parallel computing in that setting was a highly tuned, and carefully customized operation and not something you could just saunter into.

These days though, almost all computers contain multiple processors or cores on them. Even Apple's iPhone 6S comes with a dual-core CPU[1] as part of its A9 system-on-a-chip. Getting access to a "cluster" of CPUs, in this case all built into the same computer, is much easier than it used to be and this has opened the door to parallel computing for a wide range of people.

In this chapter, we will discuss some of the basic funtionality in R for executing parallel computations. In particular, we will focus on functions that can be used on *multi-core* computers, which these days is almost all computers. It is possible to do more traditional parallel computing via the network-of-workstations style of computing, but we will not discuss that here.

24.1 Hidden Parallelism

You may be computing in parallel without even knowing it! These days, many computational libraries have built-in parallelism that can be used behind the scenes. Usually, this kind of "hidden parallelism" will generally not affect you and will improve you computational efficiency. However, it's usually a good idea that you know it's going on (even in the background) because it may affect other work you are doing on the machine. Also, certain shared computing environments may have rules about how many cores/CPUs you are allowed to use and if a function fires off multiple parallel jobs, it may cause a problem for others sharing the system with you.

Parallel BLAS

A common example in R is the use of linear algebra functions. Some versions of R that you use may be linked to on optimized Basic Linear Algebra Subroutines (BLAS) library. Such libraries are custom

---
[1] https://en.wikipedia.org/wiki/Apple_A9

coded for specific CPUs/chipsets to take advantage of the architecture of the chip. It's important to realize that while R can do linear algebra out of the box, its default BLAS library is a *reference implementation* that is not necessarily optimized to any particular chipset.

When possible, it's always a good idea to install an optimized BLAS on your system because it can dramatically improve the performance of those kinds of computations. Part of the increase in performance comes from the customization of the code to a particular chipset while part of it comes from the multi-threading that many libraries use to parallelize their computations.

For example, below I simulate a matrix X of 1 million observations by 100 predictors and generate an outcome y.

```
> X <- matrix(rnorm(1e6 * 100), 1e6, 100)
> dim(X)
[1] 1000000     100
> b <- rnorm(100)
> y <- drop(X %*% b) + rnorm(1e6)
```

Then I compute the least squares estimates of the linear regression coefficents when regressing the response y on the predictor matrix X.

```
> system.time(b <- solve(crossprod(X), crossprod(X, y)))
   user  system elapsed
  0.854   0.002   0.448
```

Here, you can see that the user time is just under 1 second while the elapsed time is about half that. Here, the key task, matrix inversion, was handled by the optimized BLAS and was computed in parallel so that the elapsed time was less than the user or CPU time. In this case, I was using a Mac that was linked to Apple's Accelerate framework which contains an optimized BLAS.

Here's a summary of some of the optimized BLAS libraries out there:

- The AMD Core Math Library[2] (ACML) is built for AMD chips and contains a full set of BLAS and LAPACK routines. The library is closed-source and is maintained/released by AMD.
- The Intel Math Kernel[3] is an analogous optimized library for Intel-based chips
- The Accelerate framework[4] on the Mac contains an optimized BLAS built by Apple.
- The Automatically Tuned Linear Algebra Software[5] (ATLAS) library is a special "adaptive" software package that is designed to be compiled on the computer where it will be used. As part of the build process, the library extracts detailed CPU information and optimizes the code as it goes along. The ATLAS library is hence a generic package that can be built on a wider array of CPUs.

---

[2]http://developer.amd.com/tools-and-sdks/archive/amd-core-math-library-acml/
[3]https://software.intel.com/en-us/intel-mkl
[4]https://developer.apple.com/library/tvos/documentation/Accelerate/Reference/AccelerateFWRef/index.html
[5]http://math-atlas.sourceforge.net

Detailed instructions on how to use R with optimized BLAS libraries can be found in the R Installation and Administration[6] manual. In some cases, you may need to build R from the sources in order to link it with the optimized BLAS library.

24.2 Embarrassing Parallelism

Many problems in statistics and data science can be executed in an "embarrassingly parallel" way, whereby multiple independent pieces of a problem are executed simultaneously because the different pieces of the problem never really have to communicate with each other (except perhaps at the end when all the results are assembled). Despite the name, there's nothing really "embarrassing" about taking advantage of the structure of the problem and using it speed up your computation. In fact, embarrassingly parallel computation is a common paradigm in statistics and data science.

> In general, it is NOT a good idea to use the functions described in this chapter with graphical user interfaces (GUIs) because, to summarize the help page for `mclapply()`, bad things can happen. That said, the functions in the `parallel` package seem two work okay in RStudio.

The basic mode of an embarrassingly parallel operation can be seen with the `lapply()` function, which we have reviewed in a previous chapter. Recall that the `lapply()` function has two arguments:

1. A list, or an object that can be coerced to a list.
2. A function to be applied to each element of the list

Finally, recall that `lapply()` always returns a list whose length is equal to the length of the input list.

The `lapply()` function works much like a loop—it cycles through each element of the list and applies the supplied function to that element. While `lapply()` is applying your function to a list element, the other elements of the list are just...sitting around in memory. Note that in the description of `lapply()` above, there's no mention of the different elements of the list communicating with each other, and the function being applied to a given list element does not need to know about other list elements.

Just about any operation that is handled by the `lapply()` function can be parallelized. This approach is analogous to the "map-reduce"[7] approach in large-scale cluster systems. The idea is that a list object can be split across multiple cores of a processor and then the function can be applied to each subset of the list object on each of the cores. Conceptually, the steps in the parallel procedure are

---

[6] https://cran.r-project.org/doc/manuals/r-release/R-admin.html#BLAS
[7] https://en.wikipedia.org/wiki/MapReduce

1. Split list X across multiple cores
2. Copy the supplied function (and associated environment) to each of the cores
3. Apply the supplied function to each subset of the list X on each of the cores in parallel
4. Assemble the results of all the function evaluations into a single list and return

The differences between the many packages/functions in R essentially come down to how each of these steps are implemented. In this chapter we will cover the `parallel` package, which has a few implementations of this paradigm. The goal of the functions in this package (and in other related packages) is to abstract the complexities of the implemetation so that the R user is presented a relatively clean interface for doing computations.

24.3 The Parallel Package

The `parallel` package which comes with your R installation. It represents a combining of two historical packages–the `multicore` and `snow` packages, and the functions in `parallel` have overlapping names with those older packages. For our purposes, it's not necessary to know anything about the `multicore` or `snow` packages, but long-time users of R may remember them from back in the day.

The `mclapply()` function essentially parallelizes calls to `lapply()`. The first two arguments to `mclapply()` are exactly the same as they are for `lapply()`. However, `mclapply()` has further arguments (that must be named), the most important of which is the `mc.cores` argument which you can use to specify the number of processors/cores you want to split the computation across. For example, if your machine has 4 cores on it, you might specify `mc.cores = 4` to break your parallelize your operation across 4 cores (although this may not be the best idea if you are running other operations in the background besides R).

The `mclapply()` function (and related `mc*` functions) works via the fork mechanism on Unix-style operating systems. Briefly, your R session is the main process and when you call a function like `mclapply()`, you fork a series of sub-processes that operate independently from the main process (although they share a few low-level features). These sub-processes then execute your function on their subsets of the data, presumably on separate cores of your CPU. Once the computation is complete, each sub-process returns its results and then the sub-process is killed. The `parallel` package manages the logistics of forking the sub-processes and handling them once they've finished.

> Because of the use of the fork mechanism, the `mc*` functions are generally not available to users of the Windows operating system.

The first thing you might want to check with the `parallel` package is if your computer in fact has multiple cores that you can take advantage of.

```
> library(parallel)
> detectCores()
[1] 24
```

The computer on which this is being written is a circa 2013 Mac Pro with 2 physical CPUs, each with 6 cores. Therefore, there are 12 physical cores. However, because each core allows for hyperthreading, each core is presented as 2 separate cores, allowing for 24 "logical" cores. This is what detectCores() returns. On some systems you can call detectCores(logical = FALSE) to return the number of physical cores, but that does not appear to work on Mac OS X.

```
> detectCores(logical = FALSE)   ## Same answer?
[1] 24
```

In general, the information from detectCores() should be used cautiously as obtaining this kind of information from Unix-like operating systems is not always reliable. If you are going down this road, it's best if you get to know your hardware better in order to have an understanding of how many CPUs/cores are available to you.

mclapply()

The simplest application of the parallel package is via the mclapply() function, which conceptually splits what might be a call to lapply() across multiple cores. Just to show how the function works, I'll run some code that splits a job across 10 cores and then just sleeps for 10 seconds.

```
> r <- mclapply(1:10, function(i) {
+         Sys.sleep(10)    ## Do nothing for 10 seconds
+ }, mc.cores = 10)         ## Split this job across 10 cores
```

While this "job" was running, I took a screen shot of the system activity monitor ("top"). Here's what it looks like on Mac OS X.

```
Processes: 305 total, 3 running, 16 stuck, 286 sleeping, 1275 threads          1
Load Avg: 1.62, 1.29, 1.09  CPU usage: 4.45% user, 0.40% sys, 95.13% idle
SharedLibs: 269M resident, 22M data, 35M linkedit.
MemRegions: 51208 total, 5946M resident, 140M private, 1358M shared.
PhysMem: 15G used (3723M wired), 49G unused.
VM: 889G vsize, 529M framework vsize, 0(0) swapins, 0(0) swapouts.
Networks: packets: 2133108/2635M in, 1073520/148M out. Disks: 3040748/50G read, 1657520/59G w

PID    COMMAND     %CPU   TIME     #TH    #WQ  #PORT MEM     PURG   CMPR PGRP  PPID   STATE
22412  f951        100.2  00:06.24 1/1    0    12    303M+   0B     0B   94358 22411  running
89401  RStudio     5.7    01:07.60 44     23   331   369M+   4620K  0B   89401 1      sleeping
94299  top         2.5    00:04.97 1/1    0    44    3756K+  0B     0B   94299 72678  running
193    WindowServer 1.7   04:16.86 4      1    393   126M    4328K  0B   193   1      sleeping
1050   Terminal    1.1    02:55.46 29     23   323   67M     2732K  0B   1050  1      sleeping
0      kernel_task 0.9    12:50.30 195/24 0    2     3117M   0B     0B   0     0      running
22414  rsession    0.2    00:00.00 1      0    7     3172K   0B     0B   89401 89403  sleeping
22421  rsession    0.2    00:00.00 1      0    7     3028K   0B     0B   89401 89403  sleeping
22420  rsession    0.2    00:00.00 1      0    7     3100K   0B     0B   89401 89403  sleeping
22422  rsession    0.2    00:00.00 1      0    7     3648K   0B     0B   89401 89403  sleeping
22415  rsession    0.2    00:00.00 1      0    7     3196K   0B     0B   89401 89403  sleeping
22419  rsession    0.2    00:00.00 1      0    7     3028K   0B     0B   89401 89403  sleeping
22416  rsession    0.2    00:00.00 1      0    7     3152K   0B     0B   89401 89403  sleeping
22413  rsession    0.2    00:00.00 1      0    7     3184K   0B     0B   89401 89403  sleeping
22417  rsession    0.1    00:00.00 1      0    7     3112K   0B     0B   89401 89403  sleeping
22418  rsession    0.1    00:00.00 1      0    7     3076K   0B     0B   89401 89403  sleeping
89403  rsession    0.0    00:05.64 7      0    40    56M     0B     0B   89401 89401  sleeping
```

Multiple sub-processes spawned by mclapply()

In case you are not used to viewing this output, each row of the table is an application or process running on your computer. You can see that there are 11 rows where the COMMAND is labelled rsession. One of these is my primary R session (being run through RStudio), and the other 10 are the sub-processes spawned by the mclapply() function.

We will use as a second (slightly more realistic) example processing data from multiple files. Often this is something that can be easily parallelized.

Here we have data on ambient concentrations of sulfate particulate matter (PM) and nitrate PM from 332 monitors around the United States. First, we can read in the data via a simple call to lapply().

```
> infiles <- dir("specdata", full.names = TRUE)
> specdata <- lapply(infiles, read.csv)
```

Now, specdata is a list of data frames, with each data frame corresponding to each of the 332 monitors in the dataset.

One thing we might want to do is compute a summary statistic across each of the monitors. For example, we might want to compute the 90th percentile of sulfate for each of the monitors. This can easily be implemented as a serial call to lapply().

```
> s <- system.time({
+         mn <- lapply(specdata, function(df) {
+                 quantile(df$sulfate, 0.9, na.rm = TRUE)
+         })
+ })
> s
   user  system elapsed
  0.052   0.009   0.062
```

Note that in the system.time() output, the user time (0.052 seconds) and the elapsed time (0.062 seconds) are roughly the same, which is what we would expect because there was no parallelization.

The equivalent call using mclapply() would be

```
> s <- system.time({
+         mn <- mclapply(specdata, function(df) {
+                 quantile(df$sulfate, 0.9, na.rm = TRUE)
+         }, mc.cores = 24)
+ })
> s
   user  system elapsed
  0.130   0.217   0.049
```

Here, I chose to use 24 cores, just to see what would happen. You'll notice that the the elapsed time is now much less than the user time. However, in this case, the elapsed time is NOT 1/24th of the user time, which is what we might expect with 24 cores if there were a perfect performance gain from parallelization. R keeps track of how much time is spent in the main process and how much is spent in any child processes.

```
> s["user.self"]   ## Main process
user.self
    0.008
> s["user.child"]  ## Child processes
user.child
    0.122
```

In the call to mclapply() you can see that virtually all of the user time is spent in the child processes. The total user time is the sum of the self and child times.

In some cases it is possible for the parallelized version of an R expression to actually be *slower* than the serial version. This can occur if there is substantial overhead in creating the child processes. For example, time must be spent copying information over to the child processes and communicating the results back to the parent process. However, for most substantial computations, there will be some benefit in parallelization.

> One advantage of serial computations is that it allows you to better keep a handle on how much **memory** your R job is using. When executing parallel jobs via mclapply() it's important to pre-calculate how much memory *all* of the processes will require and make sure this is less than the total amount of memory on your computer.

The mclapply() function is useful for iterating over a single list or list-like object. If you have to iterate over multiple objects together, you can use mcmapply(), which is the the multi-core equivalent of the mapply() function.

Error Handling

When either mclapply() or mcmapply() are called, the functions supplied will be run in the sub-process while effectively being wrapped in a call to try(). This allows for one of the sub-processes to fail without disrupting the entire call to mclapply(), possibly causing you to lose much of your work. If one sub-process fails, it may be that all of the others work just fine and produce good results.

This error handling behavior is a significant difference from the usual call to lapply(). With lapply(), if the supplied function fails on one component of the list, the entire function call to lapply() fails and you only get an error as a result.

With mclapply(), when a sub-process fails, the return value for that sub-process will be an R object that inherits from the class "try-error", which is something you can test with the inherits() function. Conceptually, each child process is executed with the try() function wrapped around it. The code below deliberately causes an error in the 3 element of the list.

```
> r <- mclapply(1:5, function(i) {
+         if(i == 3L)
+                 stop("error in this process!")
+         else
+                 return("success!")
+ }, mc.cores = 5)
Warning in mclapply(1:5, function(i) {: scheduled cores 3 encountered
errors in user code, all values of the jobs will be affected
```

Here we see there was a warning but no error in the running of the above code. We can check the return value.

```
> str(r)
List of 5
 $ : chr "success!"
 $ : chr "success!"
 $ :Class 'try-error'  atomic [1:1] Error in FUN(X[[i]], ...) : error in this process!
  .. ..- attr(*, "condition")=List of 2
  .. .. ..$ message: chr "error in this process!"
  .. .. ..$ call   : language FUN(X[[i]], ...)
  .. .. ..- attr(*, "class")= chr [1:3] "simpleError" "error" "condition"
 $ : chr "success!"
 $ : chr "success!"
```

Note that the 3rd list element in r is different.

```
> class(r[[3]])
[1] "try-error"
> inherits(r[[3]], "try-error")
[1] TRUE
```

When running code where there may be errors in some of the sub-processes, it's useful to check afterwards to see if there are any errors in the output received.

```
> bad <- sapply(r, inherits, what = "try-error")
> bad
[1] FALSE FALSE  TRUE FALSE FALSE
```

You can subsequently subset your return object to only keep the "good" elements.

```
> r.good <- r[!bad]
> str(r.good)
List of 4
 $ : chr "success!"
 $ : chr "success!"
 $ : chr "success!"
 $ : chr "success!"
```

24.4 Example: Bootstrapping a Statistic

One technique that is commonly used to assess the variability of a statistic is the bootstrap. Briefly, the bootstrap technique resamples the original dataset with replacement to create pseudo-datasets that are similar to, but slightly perturbed from, the original dataset. This technique is particularly useful when the statistic in question does not have a readily accessible formula for its standard error.

One example of a statistic for which the bootstrap is useful is the median. Here, we plot the histogram of some of the sulfate particulate matter data from the previous example.

```
> dat <- read.csv("specdata/001.csv")
> sulf <- dat$sulfate
> sulf <- sulf[!is.na(sulf)]     ## Remove missing values
> hist(sulf, xlab = expression("Sulfate PM (" * mu * g/m^3 * ")"))
```

Histogram of sulf

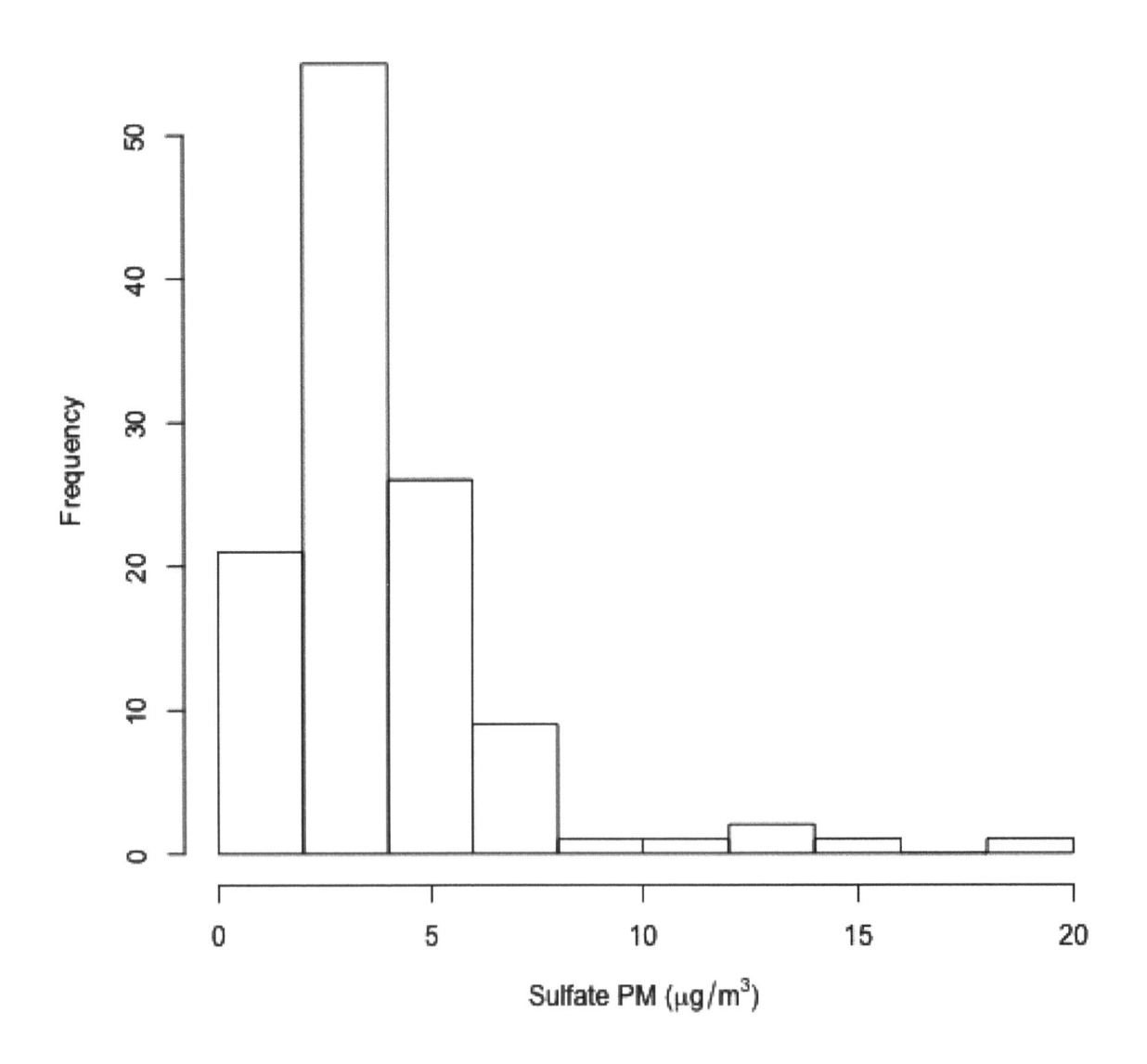

plot of chunk unnamed-chunk-14

We can see from the histogram that the distribution of sulfate is skewed to the right. Therefore, it would seem that the median might be a better summary of the distribution than the mean.

```
> summary(sulf)
   Min. 1st Qu.  Median    Mean 3rd Qu.    Max.
  0.613   2.210   2.870   3.881   4.730  19.100
```

How can we construct confidence interval for the median of sulfate for this monitor? The bootstrap is simple procedure that can work well. Here's how we might do it in the usual (non-parallel) way.

```
> set.seed(1)
> med.boot <- replicate(5000, {
+         xnew <- sample(sulf, replace = TRUE)
+         median(xnew)
+ })
```

A 95% confidence interval would then take the 2.5th and 97.5th percentiles of this distribution (this is known as the percentile method).

```
> quantile(med.boot, c(0.025, 0.975))
 2.5% 97.5%
 2.68  3.47
```

How could be done in parallel? We could simply wrap the expression passed to replicate() in a function and pass it to mclapply(). However, one thing we need to be careful of is generating random numbers.

Generating Random Numbers

Generating random numbers in a parallel environment warrants caution because it's possible to create a situation where each of the sub-processes are all generating the *exact same random numbers*. For the most part, the mc* functions do their best to avoid this.

```
> r <- mclapply(1:5, function(i) {
+         rnorm(3)
+ }, mc.cores = 5)
> str(r)
List of 5
 $ : num [1:3] -1.428 -1.765 -0.554
 $ : num [1:3] 0.0587 0.1405 -0.6107
 $ : num [1:3] -0.285 0.424 -0.561
 $ : num [1:3] 1.885 -0.512 -0.234
 $ : num [1:3] -0.754 0.252 0.446
```

However, the above expression is not **reproducible** because the next time you run it, you will get a different set of random numbers. You cannot simply call set.seed() before running the expression as you might in a non-parallel version of the code.

The parallel package provides a way to reproducibly generate random numbers in a parallel environment via the "L'Ecuyer-CMRG" random number generator. Note that this is not the default random number generator so you will have to set it explicitly.

```
> ## Reproducible random numbers
> RNGkind("L'Ecuyer-CMRG")
> set.seed(1)
> r <- mclapply(1:5, function(i) {
+         rnorm(3)
+ }, mc.cores = 5)
> str(r)
List of 5
 $ : num [1:3] -0.485 -0.626 -0.873
 $ : num [1:3] -1.86 -1.825 -0.995
 $ : num [1:3] 1.177 1.472 -0.988
 $ : num [1:3] 0.984 1.291 0.459
 $ : num [1:3] -0.621 -1.221 1.541
```

Running the above code twice will generate the same random numbers in each of the sub-processes. Now we can run our parallel bootstrap in a reproducible way.

```
> RNGkind("L'Ecuyer-CMRG")
> set.seed(1)
> med.boot <- mclapply(1:5000, function(i) {
+         xnew <- sample(sulf, replace = TRUE)
+         median(xnew)
+ }, mc.cores = 24)
> med.boot <- unlist(med.boot)   ## Collapse list into vector
> quantile(med.boot, c(0.025, 0.975))
 2.5% 97.5%
 2.70  3.46
```

> Although I've rarely seen it done in practice (including in my own code), it's a good idea to explicitly set the random number generator via RNGkind(), in addition to setting the seed with set.seed(). This way, you can be sure that the appropriate random number generator is being used every time and your code will be reproducible even on a system where the default generator has been changed.

Using the boot package

For bootstrapping in particular, you can use the `boot` package to do most of the work and the key `boot` function has an option to do the work in parallel.

```
> library(boot)
> b <- boot(sulf, function(x, i) median(x[i]), R = 5000, parallel = "multicore", ncpus = 2\
4)
> boot.ci(b, type = "perc")
BOOTSTRAP CONFIDENCE INTERVAL CALCULATIONS
Based on 5000 bootstrap replicates

CALL :
boot.ci(boot.out = b, type = "perc")

Intervals :
Level     Percentile
95%   ( 2.70,  3.47 )
Calculations and Intervals on Original Scale
```

24.5 Building a Socket Cluster

Using the forking mechanism on your computer is one way to execute parallel computation but it's not the only way that the `parallel` package offers. Another way to build a "cluster" using the multiple cores on your computer is via *sockets*. A socket[8] is simply a mechanism with which multiple processes or applications running on your computer (or different computers, for that matter) can communicate with each other. With parallel computation, data and results need to be passed back and forth between the parent and child processes and sockets can be used for that purpose.

Building a socket cluster is simple to do in R with the `makeCluster()` function. Here I'm initializing a cluster with 24 components.

```
> cl <- makeCluster(24)
```

The `cl` object is an abstraction of the entire cluster and is what we'll use to indicate to the various cluster functions that we want to do parallel computation.

> You'll notice that the `makeCluster()` function has a `type` argument that allows for different types of clusters beyond using sockets (although the default is a socket cluster). We will not discuss these other options here.

---

[8]https://en.wikipedia.org/wiki/Network_socket

To do an lapply() operation over a socket cluster we can use the parLapply() function. For example, we can use parLapply() to run our median bootstrap example described above.

```
> med.boot <- parLapply(cl, 1:5000, function(i) {
+         xnew <- sample(sulf, replace = TRUE)
+         median(xnew)
+ })
Error in checkForRemoteErrors(val): 24 nodes produced errors; first error: object 'sulf' n\
ot found
```

You'll notice, unfortunately, that there's an error in running this code. The reason is that while we have loaded the sulfate data into our R session, the data is not available to the independent child processes that have been spawned by the makeCluster() function. The data, and any other information that the child process will need to execute your code, needs to be **exported** to the child process from the parent process via the clusterExport() function. The need to export data is a key difference in behavior between the "multicore" approach and the "socket" approach.

```
> clusterExport(cl, "sulf")
```

The second argument to clusterExport() is a character vector, and so you can export an arbitrary number of R objects to the child processes. You should be judicious in choosing what you export simply because each R object will be replicated in each of the child processes, and hence take up memory on your computer.

Once the data have been exported to the child processes, we can run our bootstrap code again.

```
> med.boot <- parLapply(cl, 1:5000, function(i) {
+         xnew <- sample(sulf, replace = TRUE)
+         median(xnew)
+ })
> med.boot <- unlist(med.boot)   ## Collapse list into vector
> quantile(med.boot, c(0.025, 0.975))
 2.5% 97.5%
 2.68  3.46
```

Once you've finished working with your cluster, it's good to clean up and stop the cluster child processes (quitting R will also stop all of the child processes).

```
> stopCluster(cl)
```

24.6 Summary

In this chapter we reviewed two different approaches to executing parallel computations in R. Both approaches used the `parallel` package, which comes with your installation of R. The "multicore" approach, which makes use of the `mclapply()` function is perhaps the simplest and can be implemented on just about any multi-core system (which nowadays is any system). The "socket" approach is a bit more general and can be implemented on systems where the fork-ing mechanism is not available. The approach used in the "socket" type cluster can also be extended to other parallel cluster management systems which unfortunately are outside the scope of this book.

In general, using parallel computation can speed up "embarrassingly parallel" computations, typically with little additional effort. However, it's important to remember that splitting a computation across N processors usually does not result in a N-times speed up of your computation. This is because there is some overhead involved with initiating the sub-processes and copying the data over to those processes.

25. About the Author

Roger D. Peng is an Associate Professor of Biostatistics at the Johns Hopkins Bloomberg School of Public Health. He is also a Co-Founder of the Johns Hopkins Data Science Specialization[1], which has enrolled over 1.5 million students, the Johns Hopkins Executive Data Science Specialization[2], the Simply Statistics blog[3] where he writes about statistics and data science for the general public, and the Not So Standard Deviations[4] podcast. Roger can be found on Twitter and GitHub under the user name @rdpeng[5].

---

[1] http://www.coursera.org/specialization/jhudatascience/1
[2] https://www.coursera.org/specializations/executive-data-science
[3] http://simplystatistics.org/
[4] https://soundcloud.com/nssd-podcast
[5] https://twitter.com/rdpeng

Lightning Source UK Ltd.
Milton Keynes UK
UKHW05f2025240918
329454UK00004B/530/P